History of Louisiana

A Captivating Guide to Everything from Native Americans, Cajuns, and Creoles to the Louisiana Purchase, Battle of New Orleans, and More

Free Bonus from Captivating History (Available for a Limited time)

Hi History Lovers!

Now you have a chance to join our exclusive history list so you can get your first history ebook for free as well as discounts and a potential to get more history books for free! Simply visit the link below to join.

Captivatinghistory.com/ebook

Also, make sure to follow us on Facebook, Twitter and Youtube by searching for Captivating History.

Table of Contents

Introduction

From the Mississippi Delta to the bustling streets of New Orleans, the state of Louisiana has played pivotal roles throughout various chapters of American history. Its significance, however, extends beyond its geographical attributes or political contributions. Louisiana, with its mosaic of cultures and its strategic importance, has consistently been at the epicenter of socio-economic and political developments in North America.

With rivers serving as pathways for exploration, trade, and conflict, Louisiana was destined to become a melting pot of diversity and interests. The state's indigenous populations laid its foundational cultures long before Europeans began their explorations and settlements. The entry of the French, Spanish, and British introduced new dynamics. Each left permanent marks, from architectural styles to legal traditions, that shaped Louisiana's identity.

Native American Foundations

The history of Louisiana cannot begin without acknowledging its indigenous roots. Several tribes, most notably the Choctaw, Natchez, and Caddo, had long been inhabitants of the area, each bringing its distinct cultural, social, and economic systems.

All these tribes, despite their distinct identities, shared a profound connection to the land. This bond was not just about survival; it was about respect and reverence for the natural world. Their sustainable agricultural practices and efficient resource management provided a blueprint for ecological balance.

When European settlers began to explore and eventually settle in Louisiana, the existing knowledge and infrastructure of these tribes were indispensable. Whether it was understanding the labyrinth of waterways, recognizing edible plants, or navigating the political landscape of intertribal relations, early European settlers often relied on Native American expertise. This was a testament to the crucial and foundational role these tribes played in what Louisiana would become.

The French Imprint

The influence of the French on Louisiana's development is undeniably profound. Their involvement started with the expeditions of explorers seeking to expand France's territorial claims. Among these, Robert de La Salle stands out for his role in claiming vast stretches of North America for France, a move that had long-term geopolitical ramifications.

In the decades following La Salle's explorations, French efforts in the region became more organized and systematic. The year 1718 marked a watershed moment with the founding of New Orleans by Jean-Baptiste Le Moyne de Bienville. Over time, New Orleans, with its bustling ports and thriving markets, solidified Louisiana's status as a vital nexus for transatlantic trade.

Overall, the French epoch in Louisiana's history was multifaceted, with its legacies still palpable in the state's legal systems, cultural celebrations, and even in the rhythms of daily life. The intertwining of French colonial aspirations with the realities of the New World resulted in a unique socio-cultural milieu that distinguishes Louisiana from its neighbors.

Spanish Dominion

The mid-eighteenth-century transition of Louisiana from French to Spanish control marked a shift in the region's historical trajectory. Spain's administration, though less prolonged than its French predecessor's, instigated significant changes that have left enduring marks on Louisiana's identity.

The Spanish colonial approach differed considerably from that of the French. The Spanish emphasis was often on tighter governance and infrastructural development, aiming to consolidate control over the acquired territories. The Spanish era introduced a melding of French and Spanish civil laws, a unique legal feature of Louisiana to this day. Recognizing New Orleans' strategic importance in trade, the Spanish improved the city's port facilities. Their policies also opened trade with Spanish colonies in the Americas, further boosting the economic stature of Louisiana. Architecturally, the Spanish influence is perhaps most evident. The iconic wrought-iron balconies, courtyards, and terracotta roof tiles of the French Quarter owe their existence to Spanish aesthetics and building practices.

The period of Spanish dominion was profound in its implications. By the time the territory was retroceded to France in 1800, Spanish influence had become an integral component of Louisiana's multifaceted identity, with vestiges of its impact resonating even today.

British Presence

Though Britain's tenure in Louisiana was fleeting compared to the French and Spanish eras, its influence during this brief interlude remains noteworthy. While never directly governing the area known as the Louisiana Territory, Britain's acquisition of the region east of the Mississippi River, known as West Florida, had indirect effects on the entire region. Britain's presence in nearby territories intensified competition and necessitated geopolitical maneuvering.

British rule emphasized trade and commerce. The establishment of new trade routes and the strengthening of pre-existing ones saw Louisiana become enmeshed in a broader British Atlantic trading system. Additionally, the British brought a distinct legal perspective rooted in common law traditions. Even though this influence was subtle in Louisiana, it contributed to the region's evolving judicial landscape.

African Resilience and Legacy

African influence in Louisiana is profound, stemming primarily from the grim transatlantic slave trade but eventually blossoming into a legacy of resilience, cultural fusion, and significant societal contributions. Louisiana's agricultural economy, especially its lucrative sugar plantations, was built largely on the forced labor of enslaved Africans. Their expertise in rice cultivation and other agricultural techniques, brought from West African regions, became foundational to the state's agrarian success.

Beyond the fields, enslaved Africans brought with them a rich tapestry of cultural practices, languages, and religious beliefs. Over time, these merged with European and Native American traditions, leading to the unique Creole culture. This cultural amalgamation is most evident in Louisiana's music and cuisine, where African influences play a pivotal role.

In urban areas like New Orleans, a distinct community of free people of color began to emerge by the late eighteenth century. They played a unique role in the city's social hierarchy, navigating a space between the enslaved and the white population.

The resilience of the African community, whether in resisting the shackles of bondage or in forging a unique identity amidst adversity, remains a testament to its enduring legacy in shaping Louisiana.

In this guide, we will explore these influences and more, tracing the events and interactions that have made Louisiana a unique and vital part of the American narrative.

Chapter 1 – Pre-Colonial Period

Before the sails of European ships punctuated Louisiana's horizons, the region was home to indigenous communities, each with its own mix of traditions. This chapter seeks to peel back the layers of time, casting light on a Louisiana often overshadowed by later historical narratives. It's an area where the Choctaw, Natchez, Caddo, and other tribes shaped a colorful picture of cultures, traditions, and interactions with the land. As we delve into this period, we aim to provide a foundational understanding of the region's original inhabitants, emphasizing their contributions, intricacies, and undeniable significance in shaping the Louisiana we recognize today. This is not just a prelude but a deep exploration into the bedrock upon which all of Louisiana's history was built.

Native Tribes: A Glimpse of Original Louisiana

These weren't simply tribal communities living off the land; they were complex societies with rich traditions, governance structures, and advanced trade systems, cultivating and shaping the land many centuries before colonization. Before Europeans arrived, seven tribes made Louisiana home, including the Atakapa, Caddo, Chitimacha, Choctaw, Houma, Natchez, and Tunica. An additional four tribes joined Louisiana when they were driven there after the Europeans' arrival. These include the Alabama, Biloxi, Koasati, and Ofo. Today, only four federally recognized tribes remain in the state.

Choctaw: Traders and Mound Builders

Situated primarily in the region that spans present-day Mississippi, Louisiana, and parts of Alabama, the Choctaw nation carved out an influential space among the southeastern Native American tribes. Renowned for their agricultural prowess and remarkable trading and diplomatic skills, the Choctaw wielded considerable influence in pre-colonial America.

A Nexus of Trade and Diplomacy

The Choctaw's trading networks were nothing short of remarkable. Rather than being limited by geographical boundaries, their trading routes crisscrossed vast tracts of land, establishing them as key players in the regional exchange of goods and ideas. This vast network meant they interacted with tribes as distant as the Plains Indians in the West and the tribes of the Atlantic coast.

Their settlements often became hubs of commerce, where goods like Gulf Coast shells, Appalachian minerals, and even exotic items from distant tribes were traded. These interactions weren't merely about material exchange; they facilitated the sharing of knowledge, from agricultural techniques to spiritual beliefs. Understanding the importance of diplomacy, the Choctaw often formed alliances solidified through marriage or trade agreements, ensuring peace and mutual prosperity.

Mounds: Echoes of a Rich Cultural Heritage

To truly grasp the essence of the Choctaw civilization, one must understand the significance of their mounds. Often rising majestically from the plains, these mounds, meticulously constructed over generations, represented the heart of Choctaw communal and spiritual life.

The mounds were not just earthen structures; they encapsulated the tribe's cosmology, social structure, and political organization. Each mound had its specific purpose. Some served as platforms for the houses of the elite or the central council. Others were ceremonial centers where key religious rites were performed. The mounds also played a crucial role in the political sphere. They were venues where leaders were chosen, disputes were settled, and crucial decisions regarding the tribe's future were made.

The design and location of these mounds were not arbitrary. They were strategically positioned, often aligning with celestial bodies or events, underscoring the Choctaw's advanced knowledge of astronomy.

These alignments also had spiritual significance, connecting the earth with the heavens in their religious beliefs.

Legacy and Influence

The Choctaw's societal structures, extensive trade networks, and mound-building tradition make them one of the most influential tribes in the southeastern United States. Their legacy can be seen in the physical remnants of their civilization and in the cultural, political, and economic imprints they left on the region. Understanding the Choctaw's history and contributions offers invaluable insights into the rich tapestry of Native American cultures that thrived long before European colonization.

Natchez: Sun Worshipers and Hierarchical Society

Nestled along the fertile banks of the lower Mississippi Valley, the Natchez stood out in the rich history of southeastern tribes, even if they were the last to arrive. While the Natchez shared some characteristics with their neighbors, certain aspects of their culture, governance, and religious practices positioned the tribe as a distinct entity in the region's indigenous tapestry.

Matrilineal Society: Power and Lineage through Women

One of the standout features of the Natchez society was its matrilineal organization. In a departure from many other tribes, Natchez descent, inheritance, and societal roles were traced through the maternal line. This meant that clan identity, property rights, and even leadership roles were inherited from one's mother rather than one's father. This system underscored women's vital role in the fabric of Natchez society.

In practical terms, this meant that when a man married, he moved to his wife's household — a practice known as matrilocality. These households often consisted of extended matrilineal family members, and crucial decisions, both familial and societal, were deeply influenced by the elder women of the clan.

The Sun: Spiritual Anchor and Societal Pillar

For the Natchez, the sun was more than just a celestial entity. It was a spiritual force, a deity that cast its glow over every aspect of their lives. Daily routines, agricultural practices, and—most importantly—religious ceremonies revolved around solar patterns.

Central to their religious and political structure was the figure of the "Great Sun." Positioned as a semi-divine entity, the Great Sun was not just the paramount political leader but the chief priest, bridging the divide between the heavens and the earth. His secular and sacred decisions were absolute, guiding the destiny of the Natchez people.

Supporting the Great Sun was a hierarchical structure of lesser Suns and nobility. Each had their designated roles and responsibilities, ensuring the smooth functioning of Natchez society. This hierarchy was visually represented in their settlements. The ceremonial mounds, reminiscent of the practices of other Mississippian cultures, were more than just architectural feats. They were the residences of the Suns, symbolizing their elevated status. These mounds, especially the one reserved for the Great Sun, were venues for key religious rituals, community gatherings, and political assemblies.

The Natchez Legacy

The Natchez, with their intricate societal structures, solar veneration, and matrilineal practices, offer a fascinating study of a society that carved out a unique identity in pre-colonial America. Their legacy, while disrupted by European colonization, lives on in historical records, archaeological finds, and the oral traditions of their descendants. Delving into their history provides a glimpse into a society where the sun and the matriarchs reigned supreme, illuminating the diversity of indigenous cultures in the southeastern United States.

Caddo: Master Farmers and Ceramists

Spanning a vast region encompassing parts of present-day Arkansas, Louisiana, Oklahoma, and Texas, the Caddo tribes left an indelible mark on the historical landscape of the Southeast. Their achievements, whether in agriculture, ceramics, or community living, were a testament to their ingenuity, adaptability, and rich cultural heritage.

Agriculture: Sustenance and Stability

The foundation of the Caddo civilization lay in its mastery over agriculture. Utilizing the fertile alluvial plains to their advantage, they cultivated an array of crops that fed their population and supported their economic ventures. Prominent among these crops were the "Three Sisters"—corn, beans, and squash. This trio was more than just a dietary staple; it represented a sophisticated understanding of crop rotation, soil health, and symbiotic cultivation. Corn provided the stalks for beans to climb, beans enriched the soil with nitrogen, and squash's broad leaves minimized weed growth, creating an interdependent cycle of growth.

The success of their agricultural endeavors meant the Caddo could afford to live in settled communities rather than be nomadic. This stability translated into the establishment of permanent settlements for over 1,000 years. Central to these settlements were their distinct thatched-roof houses, constructed using locally sourced materials and designed to offer protection against the elements. Additionally, the ceremonial center mounds were religious epicenters that showcased the Caddo's societal hierarchy and architectural prowess.

Artistry in Clay: Narratives in Pottery

Beyond agriculture, the Caddo were distinguished by their exceptional skills in ceramics. Using the rich clays from the riverbanks, they crafted functional and artistically sublime pottery. Bowls, jars, and effigies bore intricate motifs and patterns, each telling a story, preserving a legend, or reflecting a spiritual belief.

This pottery was more than just household ware. It was a medium through which the Caddo chronicled their history, beliefs, and daily life. Whether it depicted a bountiful harvest, a powerful deity, or a significant tribal event, each ceramic piece was a window into the Caddo world.

The Spirit of Collective Cohesion

An interesting linguistic legacy attributed to the Caddo is the term "cahoot." Today, it signifies collaboration or working in tandem. Delving into its etymology reveals the essence of the Caddo spirit. It underscores their emphasis on communal living, collective problem-solving, and a shared destiny. For the Caddo, challenges were met head-on as a community, and successes were celebrated collectively.

European Contacts and Early Expeditions

The discovery and exploration of the New World by European powers in the sixteenth century marked a turning point in global history. The lands that would come to be known as Louisiana were no exception. These virgin territories were not just seen as lands to conquer but became the stage for geopolitical maneuvering, economic ventures, and cultural exchanges.

Spanish Footprints in the New World

The initial European forays into the region were spearheaded by the Spanish. Drawn by tales of gold-laden cities and the allure of fresh territories, Spanish conquistadors and explorers ventured north from their colonies in Central and South America. Among these explorations,

Hernando de Soto's 1541 expedition remains etched in historical records. While de Soto and his men never did find the fabled cities of gold, their travels yielded the first detailed European accounts of the Mississippi River. These accounts painted a picture of a mighty river weaving through vast and fertile lands inhabited by complex indigenous civilizations.

However, the interactions between de Soto's expedition and the indigenous populations were marred by violence and subjugation. The Spanish, with their superior weaponry and avaricious intent, often clashed with the Native tribes, leading to skirmishes, subjugation, and, unfortunately, the spread of European diseases to which the indigenous people had no immunity.

The French Intrigue and Exploration

While the Spanish expeditions were largely driven by the quest for instant wealth, the French approach to the New World, particularly in the seventeenth century, was different. Tales of vast territories crisscrossed by navigable rivers caught the imagination of French explorers and fur traders. The Mississippi River, in particular, was a potential highway into the heart of the continent, promising both economic and strategic advantages.

The interactions between the French and the indigenous tribes were markedly different from the earlier Spanish encounters. Guided by mercantile interests, especially the lucrative fur trade, the French sought alliances and trading partnerships with the tribes. The establishment of trading posts facilitated the exchange of French goods for furs, leading to a relatively cooperative relationship. However, these exchanges were not without their challenges. Differences in cultural perceptions, competition for resources, and occasional misunderstandings led to sporadic conflicts.

The Strategic Importance of Louisiana

By the late seventeenth century, the significance of Louisiana in the European colonial calculus had grown exponentially. It wasn't just another territory; it was a linchpin. Its fertile lands promised agricultural riches, its rivers provided navigable routes into the continent, and its position acted as a buffer or gateway, depending on the colonial power viewing it.

Spain, having established a vast colonial empire in the Americas, saw Louisiana as a potential buffer against English and French encroachments. For the French, Louisiana was the key to linking their Canadian holdings with the Gulf of Mexico, creating a vast north-south corridor under French control.

The Prelude to Colonial Rivalries

As the curtain came down on the seventeenth century, the stage was set for intense colonial rivalries in Louisiana. The initial explorations had revealed the region's potential, and the European powers were gearing up for a protracted contest. The explorers' interactions with the indigenous tribes had set precedents, some cooperative and others confrontational. These early contacts would shape European-Native relations in the ensuing decades.

Chapter 2 – Colonial Era

Setting the Stage for European Dominance

The colonial era in Louisiana marks a pivotal juncture in the region's history characterized by European territorial ambitions and the resulting changes imposed upon the land and its people. As European powers expanded their colonial footprints across the globe, Louisiana emerged as a key territory in the strategic and economic calculations of empires.

As we delve into this chapter, we will chronologically trace the colonial undertakings in Louisiana, from the initial French expeditions to the transitions of power between Spain and Britain. Each colonial power brought distinct administrative styles, policies, and objectives, collectively influencing the evolution of Louisiana during this period. Through a careful examination of events, policies, and key figures, we will understand how Louisiana transitioned from a region under indigenous control to one under European colonial dominance.

The French Touch: Settlements and Societal Imprints

Early Exploration and Settlements

As mentioned briefly in the last chapter, the dawn of the sixteenth century witnessed a fervent European race to explore and establish footholds in the New World. Amid this competitive backdrop, France embarked on its journey into the heart of what would become Louisiana. Initially, French explorers, like many of their European counterparts, sought elusive passages to Asia, harboring dreams of securing faster trade routes. However, the vast, untapped potential of the Mississippi River basin soon shifted these ambitions.

One cannot underscore Louisiana's French colonial narrative without highlighting the endeavors of René-Robert Cavelier, Sieur de La Salle. In 1682, leading a determined expedition, La Salle navigated the Mississippi from the Great Lakes to its delta. Grasping the strategic and economic significance of this waterway, he boldly claimed the entire river basin for France, christening it "La Louisiane" in homage to King Louis XIV.

The imprint of French commitment to Louisiana became even more pronounced with the exploits of the Le Moyne brothers, Bienville and Iberville. Recognizing the need for a permanent base, they established Fort Maurepas in 1699, marking it as France's inaugural settlement in the vast Mississippi territory, near what is today Biloxi, Mississippi. This fortified establishment symbolized France's aspirations to anchor its presence and influence. However, it was the foundation of New Orleans in 1718, primarily under Bienville's leadership, that truly solidified French colonial endeavors. Strategically positioned, New Orleans burgeoned as the heart of trade and administration, heralding a new era for French ambitions in North America.

Societal Structures and Imprints

French colonial endeavors in Louisiana were not merely driven by economic and territorial ambitions. As settlements grew, they shaped a societal framework marked by a blend of European and indigenous elements, laying the groundwork for the region's unique cultural mosaic.

The French governance model emphasized structured administration. Settlements, particularly New Orleans, were organized using a systematic urban grid, a pattern evocative of European cities. Public spaces, churches, and administrative buildings were central to these designs, emphasizing the importance of communal gatherings and religion in daily life.

Law and order were other paramount considerations. The introduction of the "Code Noir" in 1724 was particularly impactful. This legal document, instituted by King Louis XV, was a comprehensive set of regulations governing the lives of enslaved Africans and free people of color in the colony. While its primary objective was to maintain social control, it also set distinct rights and responsibilities, shaping the contours of Louisiana's budding multi-ethnic society.

The French instilled an enduring linguistic legacy. French, as the language of governance, commerce, and daily interaction, became deeply rooted. The distinct Louisiana Creole, a language born from the mingling of French with African, Spanish, and Native American tongues, further enriched the linguistic tapestry.

Religion, predominantly Catholicism, also played a defining role. The establishment of churches and missions was not just an effort to convert the indigenous populace but served as focal points for community life. They reinforced French cultural norms while providing platforms for intercultural interactions.

Trade, too, had societal implications. The fur trade, especially, fostered alliances with Native American tribes. Though often transactional, these partnerships led to cultural exchanges as French settlers adopted indigenous practices and vice versa, laying the foundation for a shared, albeit complex, colonial legacy. These exchanges, though primarily driven by economic considerations, had broader implications. They cemented relationships, forged alliances, and, at times, stoked tensions between the French settlers and the indigenous communities.

Economic Ventures and Expansion

French colonists discerned Louisiana's potential as an economic powerhouse early on. These pioneers envisioned the region not simply as a territory for extraction but as a centerpiece in the vast commercial networks of the French colonial empire.

Central to this vision was New Orleans. Its geographically strategic location along the twisting Mississippi River made it an invaluable connection for transatlantic commerce. This bustling port became the heartbeat of the colony's economic activities. From the interior regions, commodities like furs, lumber, and agricultural products flowed into New Orleans, soon to be loaded onto vessels bound for European markets. Simultaneously, European imports, from luxury textiles to essential hardware, streamed into the colony, underlining the city's significance.

Beyond the confines of the port city, Louisiana's vast arable stretches began to be tilled with purpose. Early agricultural endeavors focused on crops like indigo and tobacco, leveraging existing European demand. However, the introduction of sugarcane cultivation in the mid-eighteenth century dramatically altered Louisiana's agrarian identity. These expansive sugar plantations, bathed in the toil and sweat of enslaved Africans, rapidly emerged as key to the colony's economic framework. The rigorous and labor-intensive processes involved in sugar production solidified Louisiana's position within the transatlantic trade market.

Alongside these large-scale agricultural and commercial undertakings, the French tapped into lucrative secondary trades. The fur trade, for instance, emerged as an essential commercial activity. Utilizing an intricate network of trading posts scattered across strategic points, French traders initiated exchanges with indigenous tribes. European tools, weapons, and textiles found eager takers among the Natives, who offered valuable pelts in return.

In its entirety, the French economic strategy was a blend of ambition, adaptation, and pragmatism. By aligning their commercial pursuits with the region's natural bounties and leveraging strategic partnerships, the French successfully transformed Louisiana into an economic linchpin within their colonial dominions.

Legacy and Transition

The French era in Louisiana left an unforgettable mark, the ramifications of which resonate to this day. Its architectural contributions, most notably the charming French Quarter of New Orleans, serve as timeless reminders of France's colonial pursuits. French legal traditions also persist in Louisiana's unique civil law system, distinct from the common-law practices of other American states.

Moreover, the intricate web of relationships the French cultivated—be it with African slaves, Native tribes, or other European powers—fashioned a distinct Louisianan identity. The Creole culture, a tapestry woven with French, African, Native, and Spanish threads, exemplifies this unique convergence.

French Quarter Louisiana by llambrano.
Free for use; https://pixabay.com/service/license-summary/;
https://cdn.pixabay.com/photo/2014/12/05/03/25/french-quarter-557458_1280.jpg

Yet, as the eighteenth century drew to a close, geopolitical realities shifted. Louisiana, while crucial, was becoming a pawn in the larger game of colonial chess. The cession of the vast territory to Spain in 1762 signaled the end of the French epoch. However, the foundations laid during this period ensured that the French touch would endure in spirit and substance.

New Orleans: The Crown Jewel

The rise of New Orleans from a fledgling settlement to a colonial metropolis is one of the most pivotal narratives within Louisiana's historical tapestry. From its inception, New Orleans was envisioned as more than a mere outpost; it was to be the administrative and economic heart of the colony. The city's grid-like layout, designed by engineer Adrien de Pauger, encompassed not just streets and residences but also integrated plazas and markets, underscoring the city's intended commercial role. The Place d'Armes, today's Jackson Square, quickly became a focal point for administrative, religious, and social gatherings.

Jackson Square, formerly Place d'Armes, by USA-Reiseblogger.
Free for use; https://pixabay.com/service/license-summary/;
https://cdn.pixabay.com/photo/2016/09/01/16/59/usa-1644525_1280.jpg

New Orleans' prominence, however, wasn't simply a consequence of its strategic design or geolocation. The city's growth was inextricably tied to its diverse population. As vessels from Europe and the Caribbean docked at its ports, they brought a medley of settlers—French bureaucrats, merchants, enslaved Africans, and free people of color. This multicultural infusion endowed New Orleans with a unique socio-cultural character, creating a melting pot where European, African, and indigenous cultures converged, collaborated, and sometimes clashed.

Economically, the city's docks bustled with activity. The voluminous cargo holds of ships were loaded with Louisiana's natural bounty—timber, indigo, and, eventually, sugar—destined for European shores. In return, European wines, textiles, and other luxury goods entered the colony, catering to the burgeoning elite class of plantation owners and merchants. This constant exchange solidified New Orleans' reputation as a preeminent trade hub.

Yet, it wasn't just tangible goods that were exchanged. The city's taverns, coffee houses, and market squares reverberated with news and ideas from across the Atlantic, making New Orleans a nexus of information. French Enlightenment ideals, debates about colonial governance, and whispers of revolution from distant shores all found eager listeners in the city's streets.

However, with prosperity came challenges. As the population burgeoned, the city faced infrastructural and governance trials. Periodic floods, fires, and epidemics tested the city's resilience, highlighting the need for better urban planning and medical facilities. Additionally, the increasing population of enslaved Africans and the tensions between different ethnic groups necessitated intricate governance strategies. French colonial administrators were constantly recalibrating their approach to maintain stability.

Spanish Dominion: Changes in Governance and Lifestyle

The Treaty of Fontainebleau in 1762 and the subsequent Treaty of Paris in 1763 marked the beginning of a significant transition for Louisiana. These treaties covertly and then overtly transferred the vast territory from French to Spanish control. The change was not just symbolic; it represented a seismic shift in governance, legal structures, and societal norms.

Antonio de Ulloa was the first Spanish governor appointed to oversee this newly acquired territory. His entry into Louisiana was met with resistance from segments of the populace who were deeply entrenched in French ways. However, Spanish rule would be markedly different from French rule, and Ulloa faced the arduous task of initiating these changes amidst discernible hostility. Spain's intention was not merely to govern but to reshape Louisiana's colonial framework.

The Spanish introduced a centralized form of governance that starkly contrasted with the relatively lax French administrative approach. The Cabildo, or town council, became integral to New Orleans' governance. This body, comprising local elites, was entrusted with key decision-making powers, from urban planning to legal judgments.

Cultural and Societal Infusion

As the wheels of administration began to turn Spanish, so did the facets of daily life. Spanish dominion heralded a wave of immigrants from regions like the Canary Islands. These Isleños, as they were called, brought with them distinct customs, songs, and culinary tastes that started to infuse with the local milieu.

Architecturally, Spanish influence was undeniable. The rampant fires of 1788 and 1794, which razed significant portions of New Orleans, offered an inadvertent canvas for Spanish architectural ingenuity. The city was rebuilt with sturdier brick and mortar, embracing the iconic Spanish colonial style characterized by enclosed courtyards, ornate wrought-iron works, and balconied facades. Today's French Quarter, ironically, owes much of its aesthetic to this Spanish architectural era.

Spanish architecture, New Orleans by USA-Reiseblogger.
Free for use; https://pixabay.com/service/license-summary/;
https://cdn.pixabay.com/photo/2016/08/30/11/01/new-orleans-1630343_1280.jpg

Spanish influence was not restricted to the urban centers alone. Their rigorous town-planning methodologies birthed new settlements, each methodically plotted and structured.

Spanish Louisiana was significantly more liberal regarding the rights of free people of color. The Spanish legal system allowed for more freedoms and opportunities for manumission (legal freeing of slaves), contrasting with the stringent French Code Noir. These changing dynamics, while still rooted in colonial stratification, offered a slightly more nuanced existence for free Blacks, adding layers of complexity to the societal fabric of Louisiana.

The mixture of Spanish customs with existing French and indigenous traditions created a unique cultural tapestry. Annual festivals, market exchanges, and even religious observances started reflecting this dual heritage, making Spanish Louisiana a vibrant and dynamic colonial entity.

Economic Realignments

Under Spanish rule, Louisiana's economy began to pivot. The mercantilist policies of the Spanish Empire, though restrictive in nature, spurred some diversification. New crops, such as indigo and rice, supplemented the tobacco and fur trades. Additionally, the Spanish bolstered the local economy by rerouting a portion of the silver trade from their American colonies through New Orleans. This influx of capital reinvigorated the port city, transforming it into an essential hub for trade in the Gulf of Mexico.

Yet, there were tensions. Spanish trade laws often favored direct routes to Spain, bypassing Louisiana. This led to a surge in smuggling as local merchants sought to evade these restrictions. The unofficial trade routes, especially with British territories, underscored the adaptability of the Louisiana merchants and showcased their penchant for seeking opportunities even in restrictive conditions.

Religious Convergences

Although both the French and Spanish were predominantly Catholic, their expressions of the faith varied. Spanish colonial policies emphasized the evangelization of indigenous peoples, a mission that brought an influx of Spanish clergy to Louisiana. While adhering to Catholic dogma, these clergy introduced Spanish liturgical practices, adding another layer to the religious variety of the colony.

New Orleans and its surroundings witnessed the construction of new churches and chapels funded by Spanish coffers. Though rooted in Catholicism, the architectural designs of these edifices bore distinct Spanish influences, from their altars to their bell towers. Religious festivals, such as the Day of the Dead, began to be celebrated alongside French Catholic traditions, creating a rich blend of Iberian and Gallic religious customs.

Facing External Threats

Spanish Louisiana wasn't just faced with internal changes; the territory was constantly under the shadow of external threats, especially from the British to the east. The geopolitical significance of Louisiana made it a coveted asset.

Under Governor Bernardo de Gálvez, Spanish Louisiana faced its greatest military test. The American Revolutionary War provided a backdrop for Gálvez's campaigns, where he skillfully repelled British advances, safeguarding the territory for Spain. The Battle of Baton Rouge in 1779 was particularly noteworthy. Gálvez led a diverse force of Spaniards, Creoles, free Blacks, and Native Americans, underlining the multi-ethnic character of Spanish Louisiana's defense.

Gálvez's successful defense of the territory bolstered Spanish prestige in the region. His efforts ensured the territorial integrity of Louisiana and secured Spanish dominance in the Gulf, which would have ramifications for the geopolitical dynamics of North America for years to come.

The Twilight of Spanish Rule

The turn of the nineteenth century saw significant global shifts. European powers, embroiled in the Napoleonic Wars, recalibrated their colonial strategies in response to emerging challenges. Spain, facing internal and external pressures, found it increasingly challenging to maintain its vast overseas empire. Louisiana, a territory on the fringe of the Spanish colonial realm, was soon caught up in this geopolitical storm.

The secret Treaty of San Ildefonso in 1800 between Spain and France covertly returned Louisiana to French control. On the surface, daily life in the territory remained unchanged for a time. However, beneath this facade, unease grew among the inhabitants. They were wary of the implications of this transfer, given Napoleon Bonaparte's expansive ambitions.

This unease was not unfounded. By 1803, just three years after the covert treaty, Louisiana would once again change hands, this time sold to the United States in the famous Louisiana Purchase. The speed of these transitions reflected the changing priorities of colonial powers and showcased Louisiana's enduring strategic value.

The Lasting Legacy

Despite the relatively brief period of Spanish rule, its legacy in Louisiana is enduring. The architectural marvels of the French Quarter owe as much to Spanish design as they do to French. The intermingling of Spanish civil law traditions with French customs forged the unique legal framework Louisiana boasts today. Moreover, the cultural tapestry of Louisiana was enriched with Spanish threads. The introduction of Spanish festivals, culinary practices, and even linguistic nuances became woven into the fabric of Louisiana's diverse society. Many surnames and place names in Louisiana today bear testament to this Spanish legacy.

The British Quest for Colonial Expansion

By the mid-eighteenth century, the British Empire, having established itself as a formidable colonial power, was in a continuous struggle with France for dominance in various parts of the world. North America was one of the principal theaters of this imperial rivalry. These tensions culminated in the Seven Years' War (1756-1763), known in North

America as the French and Indian War.

The Treaty of Paris (1763) that ended the war reshaped the colonial landscape of North America. Britain received various territories, one of the most significant being the region east of the Mississippi River from France, except for New Orleans. This land, which constituted a portion of present-day Louisiana, became a part of British West Florida.

The Challenges of Governance and Assimilation

Assuming control of a newly acquired territory always posed challenges, and British West Florida was no exception. The British authorities were keen on fostering loyalty among the population, which consisted of French settlers, indigenous tribes, and a growing number of British colonists. To achieve this, they instituted a series of reforms.

One of the primary challenges was the legal system. British common law was distinct from the French and Spanish civil law traditions the locals were familiar with. To ease the transition, British officials allowed a degree of legal continuity while gradually introducing aspects of their own legal code.

Religion, too, was a matter of contention. The majority Catholic population, accustomed to religious freedom under previous administrations, found themselves under a Protestant empire. British policy, however, proved accommodating. Instead of imposing the Church of England as the sole religious authority, the British permitted Catholicism to continue, though it did not enjoy the same privileged status it once held.

Trade practices and alliances with indigenous tribes also required delicate navigation. The British recognized the importance of maintaining good relations with Native American tribes, a lesson they had learned from previous colonial endeavors. Thus, they continued the tradition of gift-giving ceremonies and honored existing trade agreements while forging new alliances.

This early phase of British rule, while marked by challenges, showcased the empire's adaptability and intent to integrate Louisiana into its broader colonial framework.

Economic Expansion and Infrastructure

British West Florida, though relatively modest in size, became a key focal point in Britain's North American economic strategy. The British Crown recognized the region's potential, especially given its access to the

Gulf of Mexico and the Mississippi River. Soon, initiatives were put in place to develop ports, boost trade, and exploit the area's natural resources.

Timber and naval stores became prime exports, with pine forests proving especially lucrative. Additionally, the British sought to diversify agricultural production. While indigo and tobacco were previously dominant under French rule, the British introduced rice and cotton, foreseeing the future profitability of these commodities. This diversification augmented the region's economic robustness and began to change the nature of labor, especially with the rising demand for enslaved labor on cotton plantations.

Infrastructure also saw improvements. Roads and forts were built or enhanced to facilitate better communication and defense. The port of Pensacola, in particular, was expanded and fortified, reinforcing its status as a crucial maritime hub in the Gulf.

End of British Rule and Legacy

However, British control over West Florida was short-lived. The American Revolutionary War, which erupted in 1775, shifted Britain's focus away from its southern colonies. By 1781, Spanish forces had recaptured Pensacola, and in the subsequent Treaty of Paris (1783), Britain ceded West Florida back to Spain.

Despite the brevity of British rule, their influence in Louisiana was marked. Their efforts to diversify the economy laid the groundwork for future agricultural and trade practices. Furthermore, the British approach to governance, which often emphasized pragmatism and adaptability, provided lessons for subsequent rulers. While the British era in Louisiana's history was but a fleeting moment, it symbolized the broader ebb and flow of colonial ambitions in North America.

Chapter 3 – The Louisiana Purchase

The Louisiana Purchase of 1803 stands as one of the most significant land acquisitions in US history. This transaction, facilitated between the United States and France, essentially doubled the territorial size of the young nation. But beyond the vast expanse of land, the purchase held deeper ramifications for both domestic and foreign policies.

This chapter will examine the geopolitical context leading to the Louisiana Purchase, the negotiations that cemented the deal, and the subsequent challenges and implications of integrating this vast territory into the United States.

The Geopolitical Playground: Napoleon and America

By the beginning of the nineteenth century, the international stage was struggling with a war between tensions and ambitions. Central to this was the sudden rise of Napoleon Bonaparte in France. Having staged a coup in 1799, Napoleon was rapidly reshaping the European map, aiming for continental dominance. His ambitions, however, extended beyond Europe, with the Americas presenting opportunities and challenges for his grand vision.

While the French had lost significant territories to Britain in the Seven Years' War, most notably Canada, they still held high hopes in the Caribbean and North America. The sugar colonies in the Caribbean were especially lucrative and strategic for the French economy. In North America, Louisiana held not just land but control over the Mississippi

River, a crucial artery for trade.

In this context, the secret Treaty of San Ildefonso in 1800 took place. This move was orchestrated by Napoleon with a clear aim: to reestablish a mighty French empire in the West. He envisioned a colonial system that could provide resources to fuel the French mainland and create a counterbalance against British naval dominance.

However, Napoleon's vision was not without its challenges. The French faced insurrections in Saint-Domingue (modern-day Haiti), a critical Caribbean colony. Led by Toussaint L'Ouverture, this successful slave revolt diverted French resources and attention, draining military and economic capital earmarked for North American endeavors. The situation was further worsened by yellow fever, which decimated the ranks of the French troops sent to quell the rebellion. As a result, Napoleon's dream of a revived Caribbean empire started to fade.

Parallel to this, under President Thomas Jefferson, the United States was undergoing its own expansionist ambitions. The Mississippi River, and more crucially, the port of New Orleans, was vital for the economic interests of the growing nation. Western farmers and merchants depended on the river to transport their goods. When reports reached the US administration that the Spanish might transfer control of this vital region to the French, alarm bells rang. The prospect of the ambitious Napoleon controlling the mouth of the Mississippi was a scenario that Jefferson and his advisors wanted to avoid at all costs.

Jefferson initially aimed for a more limited acquisition. He sent envoys to Paris with the mandate to purchase New Orleans and, if possible, the lands east of the Mississippi. Little did he anticipate the broader offer that would soon be on the table.

As France grappled with its setbacks in the Caribbean and an impending war on European soil and the US sought to secure its western frontier and trade routes, the wheels began to turn.

In Paris, the United States envoys, James Monroe and Robert R. Livingston, faced a mixture of diplomatic uncertainty and opportunity. French foreign minister Charles Maurice de Talleyrand, acting on Napoleon's behalf, made the surprising offer to sell not just New Orleans but the entire Louisiana territory. The vast expanse of this land stretched from the Mississippi River to the Rocky Mountains and from the Gulf of Mexico to Canada. This was a territory rich in resources and potential and encompassed land vital to America's expansionist dreams.

From a monetary standpoint, the asking price of $15 million, equating to approximately four cents an acre, was a relatively modest sum for such a vast tract of land. However, the political implications were monumental. Accepting this deal meant that the United States would double its territorial size, solidify control over the Mississippi River, and remove the immediate threat of European interference in its westward expansion.

For Napoleon, the sale was a pragmatic move. It ensured that Louisiana would not fall into British hands in the event of war, and the financial proceeds could be used to bolster the French treasury, which had been strained by his various military campaigns. More importantly, Napoleon believed that a strengthened United States could serve as a commercial and political counterweight to Britain.

This sale was not without its controversies. In the US, constitutional purists debated whether the federal government had the authority to acquire such a vast territory. Jefferson, a strict interpreter of the Constitution, was torn between the legal challenges and the undeniable strategic benefits of the purchase. However, recognizing the unique opportunity at hand, he ultimately chose pragmatism over strict constitutional adherence. Congress ratified the purchase treaty in October 1803.

In France, some lamented the loss of a potential North American empire. They viewed the sale as a concession of French ambitions in the New World. Yet, given the complexities of the European political landscape and the challenges in the Caribbean, many in the French political establishment acknowledged the wisdom in Napoleon's decision.

For Europe, the transaction marked a reconfiguration of colonial ambitions. Having divested its holdings in mainland North America, France shifted its focus towards other colonial endeavors in Africa and Asia. The Louisiana Purchase signaled a transition in the geopolitical balance, emphasizing the rise of the United States as a formidable player on the international stage.

The Deal That Changed a Nation

The Louisiana Purchase is often heralded in American history as a masterstroke of diplomacy and vision, even if it could be attributed to luck rather than ingenuity. But beyond its political significance, the deal reshaped the internal fabric of the young United States. This set in motion a series of changes that would redefine the nation's identity, demographics, and even destiny.

Land and Settlement

The acquisition of the vast Louisiana territory provided the promise of future settlement and development. While the eastern seaboard was becoming increasingly populated and industrialized, this new land offered the prospect of agricultural expansion. The concept of the American frontier, previously confined to the Appalachian Mountains, now shifted westward.

The vast territory was largely uncharted by Americans. Expeditions, like the famed Lewis and Clark journey, were commissioned to explore, map, and establish an American presence throughout the new lands. These explorations yielded invaluable information about the region's geography, indigenous communities, flora, and fauna, paving the way for future settlers.

Settling these lands was not without its challenges. Existing indigenous populations, such as the Osage and the Pawnee, had longstanding claims to these territories. Their cultures and societies, deeply rooted in the landscapes of the Great Plains, would come into direct conflict with American expansionist ambitions.

Infrastructure and Economy

The Mississippi River, the lifeline of the new territory, underwent a transformation in the post-purchase period. Previously a route for explorers and trappers, it rapidly became a bustling artery for commerce. The city of St. Louis, strategically positioned at the confluence of the Mississippi and Missouri Rivers, emerged as a vital inland port, facilitating trade between the agricultural heartland and the eastern cities.

Moreover, the territory's rich natural resources spurred economic ventures. Timber from the vast forests, minerals from the Ozark plateau, and, eventually, the discovery of gold in the western fringes fueled economic booms in specific sectors. The purchase diversified its economic base, reducing dependency on the Atlantic seaboard's industries.

Cultural Impacts

The cultural implications of the Louisiana Purchase were profound. The new territories brought a rich tapestry of French and Spanish influences into the Union. In cities like New Orleans and St. Louis, architecture, cuisine, music, and language bore testament to their colonial legacies. Creole and Cajun communities, with their unique blend of French, African, Spanish, and Native American heritages, added a distinct flavor to the American cultural mosaic.

Furthermore, as settlers from the eastern states moved westward, they carried traditions, values, and aspirations that often melded with or confronted the existing cultural norms of the newly acquired territories. This mixture and sometimes friction of cultures set the stage for a unique American identity that was continually evolving and adapting.

Legal and Political Repercussions

The vastness of the Louisiana territory posed a significant challenge to the American administrative and legal framework. How would this land be governed? Would it be carved into new states or remain territories? These questions brought the issue of states' rights versus federal authority to the forefront, a debate that would persist for decades.

Moreover, the question of slavery became increasingly contentious. The Missouri Compromise of 1820, an agreement that solidified the status of slavery in the new states carved out of the Louisiana Purchase, was a temporary solution to a growing national split. Maintaining the balance between slaveholding and free states, directly linked to the land acquired in the purchase, would become a central issue leading up to the Civil War.

A Legacy Etched in History

The Louisiana Purchase is not just a transaction etched in history books; it is a seminal moment that redefined the trajectory of a nation. It bolstered the United States' position as a dominant force in North America, ensuring its influence would stretch from sea to shining sea. The challenges, conflicts, and opportunities that arose from this acquisition shaped the character, values, and ambitions of the American people.

In retrospect, the Louisiana Purchase is a testament to visionary leadership, adept diplomacy, and a relentless pursuit of national interest. It underscores the dynamism of a young nation, eager to expand its horizons and willing to navigate the uncharted waters of geopolitics and internal governance. In many ways, the contours of modern America were sketched in the bold strokes of the Louisiana Purchase agreement.

Westward Dreams: Implications and Impact

When President Thomas Jefferson secured the Louisiana Purchase, the American populace beheld a vast and uncharted wilderness before them, a terrain rife with potential and fraught with challenges. This expansive terrain represented a new frontier, a literal and metaphorical West that beckoned with the allure of uncharted horizons. For many, it embodied the quintessential American dream—unlimited possibility. The purchase was more than a land deal; it was a siren call to adventurers, pioneers, and those in search of a fresh start.

One cannot underestimate the magnetism of this untouched expanse for the average American of that era. While prosperous, the East had its social hierarchies, its defined plots of land, and its well-trodden paths. But the West? It was the realm of the unknown. In the eyes of many, it was akin to a blank canvas waiting for the brushstrokes of exploration, cultivation, and civilization. This unspoiled wilderness offered space, resources, and an invitation to shape one's destiny. To own a piece of land, to cultivate it, and to pass it down to one's progeny was a compelling aspiration fundamental to the ethos of many early Americans.

Moreover, the idea of westward expansion was not just about individual aspirations; it was intrinsically tied to the burgeoning nation's identity. The concept of "Manifest Destiny"—the belief that Americans were divinely ordained to expand across the continent—gained traction during this period. This ideology, while controversial, resonated with a significant portion of the populace and was often used to justify the rapid colonization of the West.

The narratives spun around the West, from the tales of fur trappers to the diaries of pioneers, added to its mystique. Stories of vast plains teeming with buffalo, towering mountain ranges gleaming with snow, and rivers that meandered like serpents through verdant valleys filled the public imagination. These tales, sometimes embellished, painted a picture of a land ripe for conquest. For the more entrepreneurially inclined, tales of gold in California represented an opportunity to amass significant wealth.

In essence, the West, as conceived in the aftermath of the Louisiana Purchase, was a landscape of dreams—some realized, some shattered, but all indelibly etched into the fabric of the nation. It was a chapter where the ideals of freedom, enterprise, and Manifest Destiny jostled with the realities of indigenous dispossession and the often harsh challenges of frontier life. The story of westward expansion is thus not just a chronicle of territorial growth but a nuanced tapestry of hope, ambition, conflict, and resilience.

Economic Paradigm Shift

Before the Louisiana Purchase, the US economy was largely anchored in the eastern seaboard cities. Commerce rooted in transatlantic trade and agricultural endeavors in the hinterlands characterized this economic landscape. However, the purchase opened a veritable treasure trove of resources. The fertile plains of the Midwest, rich in nutrients, held the promise of agricultural bounty. These vast stretches of land became attractive destinations for settlers seeking to cultivate crops and establish family homesteads. As farming communities proliferated, the Midwest transformed into the nation's breadbasket, supplying domestic markets and creating export opportunities.

Yet, agriculture was just one piece of the economic puzzle. The region, abundant in minerals, timber, and other natural resources, attracted speculators and industrialists. Mines were dug, forests were felled, and industries sprouted around these endeavors. Towns burgeoned around mines and mills, and an intricate web of trade routes evolved, connecting these new centers of activity to eastern markets and international ports.

Social Reconfigurations

The westward movement was not solely an economic phenomenon; it had profound social implications. The frontier presented a canvas of opportunity, often romanticized as a place where one could reinvent oneself, free from the rigid class structures of the East. This sentiment resonated deeply with immigrants arriving in the US, many of whom saw the West as a haven to carve out a new life. Consequently, the regions acquired through the purchase became melting pots of diverse ethnicities, cultures, and traditions.

However, this westward expansion also brought settlers into closer contact (and often conflict) with the indigenous tribes of the region. Native American communities, with their own rich tapestries of traditions, were increasingly marginalized. Their ancestral lands were infringed upon, and treaties were disregarded or coercively renegotiated. This period was marred by a series of confrontations, negotiations, and forced relocations that would leave lasting scars on the nation's conscience.

Chapter 4 – Antebellum Period

The Antebellum Period is a period in history that spans from the early nineteenth century to the outbreak of the Civil War in 1861. In Louisiana, it begins with statehood in 1812 and ends with the state joining the Confederacy in 1860. This period stands among the most changing and conflicting eras in American history. Characterized by rapid economic growth, significant territorial expansion, and profound cultural and societal shifts, this moment in Louisiana's history was far more transformative than most are taught to believe. Beneath the surface of prosperity and expansion, deep-seated tensions developed, primarily centered on the institution of slavery, which would eventually plunge the nation into its bloodiest conflict.

After acquiring the Louisiana Territory, the United States continued to stretch its borders westward and southward. This territorial growth was both a cause for celebration and a source of friction. As new states sought admission to the Union, the perennial question reemerged: would they be slaveholding or free? The delicate balance of power in Congress hinged on the answer to this question.

Economically, the Antebellum Period witnessed an industrial boom in the North and a surge in cotton production in the South, facilitated by the forced labor of enslaved Africans. The invention of the cotton gin in 1793 made cotton a much more profitable commodity. The subsequent boom in the cotton industry embedded the institution of slavery even deeper into the Southern economy and way of life. As Northern states began to industrialize and urbanize, advocating for a different economic model, the divide between the agriculturalist South and the industrial North became increasingly pronounced.

Field of cotton by Valdosta.
*Free for use; https://pixabay.com/service/license-summary/;
https://cdn.pixabay.com/photo/2013/12/26/13/39/cotton-233920_1280.jpg*

The Antebellum Period was a time of great innovation and evolution, marking a rise in distinct American literary, artistic, and philosophical movements. Transcendentalists like Ralph Waldo Emerson and Henry David Thoreau wrote of individualism and a deeper relationship with nature. Writers such as Harriet Beecher Stowe used their skills with words to challenge the moral foundations of slavery, pushing the national conversation to a boil.

Social reforms also marked the era. The temperance movement, women's suffrage, and educational reforms all came to the forefront, reflecting a society grappling with its identity and values. Beneath all this, the shadow of slavery loomed, leading to heightened tensions and fierce debates in the government, economy, and among the general populace.

In studying the Antebellum Period, we are not only tracing the trajectory of a nation on the brink of war. We are exploring an entire society in flux, a nation attempting to define its ethos while wrestling with its most significant moral quandary. The decisions made, the tensions exacerbated, and the battles of this period—both ideological and physical—irrevocably shaped the American narrative for centuries to come.

Plantations and the Shadows of Slavery

During the Antebellum Period, Louisiana bore the dual marks of incredible economic growth and profound moral contradictions. The backbone of its prosperity, the sprawling plantations, became symbols of both wealth and inhumanity. The vast fields of sugar and cotton that painted the Louisiana landscape were tilled and maintained on the backs of enslaved individuals whose lives, freedoms, and rights were forfeited to perpetuate an economic system.

At the heart of this system lay the plantation economy. Plantations were not merely agricultural enterprises; they were complex communities in and of themselves. Owners or planters, who could be white or free black, often held significant power, not just over their lands but within the broader socio-political landscape of Louisiana. Their wealth granted them considerable influence in local and state politics.

These plantations, particularly in southern Louisiana, predominantly focused on sugar cultivation. The Mississippi River's rich alluvial soil proved ideal for this crop. By the mid-nineteenth century, Louisiana was responsible for the vast majority of sugar produced in the United States. Sugar cultivation was a labor-intensive process, and planters sought to maximize their profits by minimizing labor costs, leading to the purchase and exploitation of more enslaved individuals.

Parallel to the sugar plantations were the equally expansive cotton farms. These were more prevalent in the uplands and the northern reaches of Louisiana. Cotton, dubbed "white gold" by some, became an integral part of the American and European textile industries. Like sugar, cotton cultivation demanded intensive labor, and this demand was met through the institution of slavery.

However, the plantation system was more than just fields and crops. It encompassed an entire societal structure. At the top were the planters and their families, living in grand homes. These homes, often architectural marvels, were designed to showcase the wealth and prestige of their owners. Yet, merely a stone's throw away, one would find the enslaved quarters—a stark contrast in their simplicity and functionality. The proximity of these two worlds—a world of luxury and a world of forced servitude—was a daily reminder of the gross disparities underpinning Louisiana's economic success.

The lives of the enslaved were dictated by a regimen of hard work, discipline, and deprivation. Their days began before sunrise and extended until after sunset, with little reprieve. They were subjected to the urges and desires of their owners, and any resistance or defiance was met with harsh punishment. Yet, within these confines, the enslaved sought to carve out a sense of community and identity. They developed a distinct culture, blending African traditions with those they encountered in Louisiana. Music, dance, and spiritual practices became avenues of expression, solace, and resistance.

The plantation system, for all its economic success, was an institution built on contradictions. While it propelled Louisiana to the forefront of American agricultural production, it did so at a tremendous human cost. The shadows cast by these grand plantations were long and dark, filled with the stories of those who toiled under the oppressive Louisiana sun, dreaming of freedom and equality.

As the plantation system flourished, so did the cities and ports that supported this burgeoning economy. New Orleans, already an important commercial hub, witnessed further growth as sugar and cotton flowed through its docks, destined for markets across the nation and the Atlantic. The city's economic prominence translated to political power, with planters and their commercial allies playing pivotal roles in shaping state policies and laws.

Central to this economic matrix was the slave trade. New Orleans now claimed the title of one of the largest slave markets in the country. Enslaved individuals were auctioned off in the heart of the city, their worth determined by age, health, and skills. Families were often torn apart, with children, parents, and spouses sold to different owners. The human tragedy that unfolded within these marketplaces is a haunting legacy of the Antebellum Period in Louisiana.

The institution of slavery also birthed a complex societal hierarchy, even within the enslaved community. The enslaved who worked within the plantation house—cooks, maids, and valets—often had different experiences compared to those who toiled in the fields. They might have had better clothing and food, but they were under the constant surveillance of the planter's family, with little privacy or freedom of movement. Field workers, on the other hand, faced the brunt of the physical labor, exposed to the elements and the ever-present threat of the overseer's whip.

The stability of the plantation system and its societal structures was a mirage and began to face challenges as the nineteenth century progressed. The moral and ethical implications of slavery became a hot-blooded topic. It stole the stage, not just in Louisiana but across the United States. The abolitionist movement in the North grew stronger, advocating for the immediate end of slavery. Abolitionist publications, testimonies, and activism put the Southern states, including Louisiana, on the defensive.

In Louisiana, the tension was palpable. The economy of the state had a significant stake in the concept of the plantation and, by extension, the institution of slavery. Planters argued for pro-slavery since their way of life depended on the enslaved workforce. They argued for the "positive good" theory of slavery, claiming it was a civilizing institution for the African "savages." These justifications starkly contrasted with the everyday realities of the enslaved people, who continuously resisted their conditions through acts of defiance, escapes, and even revolts.

By the brink of the Civil War, Louisiana's Antebellum society found itself at a crossroads. The coming conflict would challenge the very foundations of this society, forcing Louisiana to reckon with its legacy and determine its future path.

Cultural Infusions: European and African Interplay

In the unique tapestry of Louisiana's history, one of the most profound threads is the cultural interplay between European settlers and the African population. This interaction, marked by both conflict and collaboration, gave rise to a unique Louisiana Creole culture that combined European, African, and indigenous traditions.

While the European footprint was significant, the forced migration of African populations to Louisiana would prove the most transformative. The transatlantic slave trade, driven by the insatiable demand for labor on plantations, transported thousands of Africans from various regions and ethnic groups to Louisiana. These individuals brought a wealth of traditions, languages, religious practices, and knowledge that would fundamentally shape Louisiana's cultural milieu.

One of the earliest and most visible markers of this interplay was the development of the Louisiana Creole language. This hybrid tongue, formed mainly from French but also containing elements of African and indigenous languages, facilitated communication in a multi-ethnic society. It became a lingua franca for both the enslaved population and their European masters, especially in plantation settings. Over time, it evolved and solidified, reflecting the fusion of cultures in the region.

Religion became another domain where European and African traditions melded. While Catholicism was the predominant faith introduced by European settlers, the enslaved Africans often practiced indigenous African religions. Over time, as conversion efforts intensified, many enslaved individuals adopted Catholicism, but not without infusing it with their own beliefs. This syncretism gave birth to unique religious practices in which Catholic saints became associated with African deities. Rituals, music, and even places of worship reflected this intertwined religious identity.

Music and dance, crucial components of both European and African cultures, also witnessed remarkable fusion in Louisiana. African rhythms, instruments, and dance forms met European melodies and instruments, giving rise to distinct musical genres. The early precursors of jazz, a genre synonymous with Louisiana and especially New Orleans, can be traced back to this blend. Enslaved Africans, using music as a form of expression and resistance, combined European instruments like the violin with African drums, creating sounds that transcended boundaries.

Additionally, the culinary landscape of Louisiana was significantly enriched by this cultural exchange. While European settlers introduced their methods of cooking and certain ingredients, African culinary knowledge played an essential role in shaping Louisiana's iconic dishes. Gumbo, a staple of Louisiana cuisine, is a testament to this. Its very name derives from the West African word for okra, *ki ngombo*, a primary ingredient. African methods of cooking, combined with available European and Native ingredients, resulted in a culinary tradition that stood out in the broader American South.

In the sphere of law and governance, the Code Noir established by the French and later adopted and altered by the Spanish dictated the status and treatment of slaves. However, within these constraints, the enslaved and free Africans often found loopholes and opportunities to assert their rights and create spaces for autonomy.

While music, language, religion, and cuisine are often celebrated dimensions of the European-African interplay, other subtler yet impactful areas of exchange merit attention. This cultural fusion greatly influenced the realms of arts and crafts, societal structures, festivals, and even agricultural practices.

In the realm of arts and crafts, quilting emerged as a significant medium of expression. Quilts, initially a practical item, became canvases upon which stories, histories, and aspirations were embroidered. African motifs and symbols were interwoven with European designs, creating practical and extremely meaningful textiles. These quilts often served dual purposes as decorative items and subtle communication tools, especially among the enslaved population.

Societal structures in Antebellum Louisiana also bore the mark of this cultural interplay. The emergence of the *gens de couleur libres*, or "free people of color," especially in urban areas like New Orleans, presented a unique dimension to Louisiana's societal fabric. Often of mixed European and African heritage, this group occupied a complex social position. They owned property, received formal education, and even owned slaves in certain instances. Their presence challenges monolithic understandings of race and class during this period.

Festivals and public celebrations became a stage upon which European and African traditions could visibly meld. Mardi Gras, one of the most iconic festivals associated with Louisiana today, especially New Orleans, was heavily influenced by both European carnival traditions and African dance and music. Masking and parade traditions within Mardi Gras, particularly the Mardi Gras Indians, showcase a blend of African, Native American, and European influences.

Agriculture, the backbone of Louisiana's antebellum economy, was not immune to this cultural blending. While plantation owners and European settlers brought knowledge of European farming techniques, the enslaved Africans contributed their agricultural knowledge, learned over generations in diverse African climates. Rice cultivation, for instance, benefited from the expertise of enslaved Africans from rice-growing regions of West Africa. Their knowledge in irrigation, planting, and harvesting proved invaluable. The cultivation of indigo, another major cash crop, was similarly influenced by African expertise.

It is essential to understand that this cultural interplay wasn't always harmonious. The oppressive backdrop of slavery meant that many of these exchanges happened in environments of significant power imbalance. Enslaved Africans, facing cultural erasure, had to navigate a delicate balance of preserving their traditions while also adapting to the dominant European culture. This resistance, adaptation, and fusion happened simultaneously, creating layers of complexity.

However, in the midst of this oppressive environment, moments of resistance and subversion emerged. The 1811 German Coast Uprising, the largest slave revolt in US history, was a stark example. Inspired by the Haitian Revolution and disillusioned by the harsh realities of plantation life, the enslaved Africans revolted, signaling their refusal to be subjugated. Although the revolt was quelled, it left an unforgettable mark on Louisiana's history and became a testament to the indomitable spirit of the enslaved.

Moreover, the establishment of maroon communities, settlements of runaway slaves in the swamps and woodlands of Louisiana, was another symbol of resistance. These communities, often isolated from society, became pockets where African traditions could be preserved and practiced without the direct oversight of European masters.

Toward Civil Unrest: Louisiana's Dilemma

Continuing through the nineteenth century, the United States found itself caught in intense debates over the institution of slavery, states' rights, and economic gaps between the industrial North and the rural South. Louisiana was thrust into the heart of this turmoil.

The fertile lands provided by the Mississippi River and its tributaries, had made Louisiana one of the richest states in the South. However, this prosperity came at a grave moral cost, as it was built on the backs of enslaved Africans. As Northern states moved towards industrialization and reduced reliance on slavery, Louisiana and its Southern counterparts dug their heels in, defending what they viewed as their "peculiar institution."

The intricacies of Louisiana's social fabric added layers of complexity to its position. The presence of the *gens de couleur libres* defied simplistic Northern assumptions about race relations in the South. Simultaneously, the existence of this class did not negate the systemic oppression faced by the vast majority of black Louisianans.

As abolitionist sentiments grew stronger in the North, Louisiana found its economic interests directly threatened. The cotton industry was deeply reliant on the labor-intensive cultivation methods that only seemed feasible through the continuation of slavery. Adding to the complexity, Louisiana's bustling port city, New Orleans, became a hub for trade and cultural exchange. While it profited immensely from the sale of cotton and other cash crops, the city was also exposed to ideas and perspectives from beyond the South, including anti-slavery sentiments.

By the 1850s, Louisiana was grappling with these dichotomies on both political and societal fronts. In response, the state passed more stringent slave codes. These were designed to further restrict the rights of both enslaved and free black individuals in a bid to solidify the institution of slavery. At the same time, the state's representatives in Congress found themselves at the center of heated debates over issues like the spread of slavery into new territories and states' rights.

Internally, Louisiana was anything but uniform in its views. While the minority plantation-owning elite wielded significant power and were vociferously pro-slavery, a sizable group, especially small farmers and urban dwellers, did not own slaves and held more nuanced views on the institution. For these individuals, economic concerns, such as tariffs and trade policies, often held as much significance as the question of slavery.

As the Antebellum Period drew to a close and the Civil War approached, events like the Dred Scott decision of 1857 (which effectively ruled that Congress couldn't prohibit slavery in the territories) and John Brown's raid on Harpers Ferry in 1859 only intensified these divisions even within pro-slave states. The election of Abraham Lincoln in 1860, perceived by many in Louisiana as a direct threat to the Southern way of life, brought matters to a head.

In retrospect, Louisiana's journey from 1850 to 1865 was marked by profound transformations. The "dilemma" it faced wasn't just about secession or allegiance but about its very identity. As the state grappled with external pressures and internal divisions, the choices made had lasting implications, redefining Louisiana's place in the Union and reshaping its societal landscape for generations to come.

Chapter 5 – Civil War and Reconstruction

The American Civil War, spanning from 1861 to 1865, remains a profound chapter in our nation's collective memory. With its lifeblood coursing through the mighty Mississippi River, Louisiana was not merely a backdrop to this historical drama but its stage. Its strategic location and rich cultural fabric made Louisiana indispensable to the Southern cause. The state's significance, whether through commerce, geography, or shared Southern identity, cannot be understated when reflecting upon this conflict-driven period. Its decision to secede from the Union and subsequent experiences during the war and Reconstruction illuminate broader themes of conflict, identity, and transformation.

This chapter delves deep into Louisiana's journey during these tumultuous years. From the secession debate, which exposed the state's internal divisions, to the brutal theaters of war on its soil and the daunting task of post-war rebuilding, Louisiana's story offers a nuanced story of a region in turmoil.

Choosing Sides: The Secession Question

Louisiana's position in the antebellum South was unique. By 1860, enslaved individuals constituted nearly half of Louisiana's population, firmly entwining the state's economy with the system of forced labor. This interdependence with slavery aligned many of Louisiana's interests with the broader Southern cause.

New Orleans, vibrant and diverse, has historically been a crossroads of cultures, tongues, and global economic pursuits. The city's web of commerce reached far corners of the world, making its traders as intertwined with the markets of the North as they were with the South's sprawling landscapes. Such economic ties to the North added layers of complexity to the already heated debates around secession. Unionist sentiments were not uncommon, particularly in northern parishes, especially those with fewer enslaved individuals, and among those who foresaw the devastating economic ramifications of a split from the Union. Reports of hostility towards secessionist recruiters in these areas hinted at the underlying fractures within the state.

As national tensions mounted, especially following the contentious election of Abraham Lincoln in 1860, the secession debate reached a fever pitch within Louisiana. Local newspapers became arenas for passionate arguments from both sides. Unionist editorials often highlighted the state's economic ties to the North and warned of the catastrophic consequences of war. Secessionists, on the other hand, painted a picture of a Southern utopia, free from Northern interference, where states' rights and the institution of slavery would be preserved.

Public assemblies, town hall meetings, and informal gatherings further fueled the debate. While the elite planter class, whose wealth was deeply tied to the slave economy, largely championed the Confederate cause, many small farmers, merchants, and urban residents remained wary of severing ties with the Union. The decision was further complicated by Louisiana's diverse ethnic makeup, including a sizable population of Creoles and free people of color, whose loyalties and interests did not always align neatly with either the Unionist or secessionist camps.

By January 1861, the pressure to make a decision had become untenable. The state's political machinery swung into action, calling for a convention to determine Louisiana's course. Delegates from across the state convened in Baton Rouge, faced with the monumental task of deciding Louisiana's allegiance.

The city was rife with apprehension. The nation watched closely, aware that Louisiana's decision could sway other border states. Within the convention's walls, the weight of the responsibility was palpable. While many delegates arrived with pre-formed stances, others were genuinely torn, representing constituencies with diverse concerns and interests.

Secessionist voices were dominant from the outset. Numerous proponents presented their case grounded in the defense of state rights and maintaining the Southern lifestyle. Foremost in their considerations was safeguarding slavery, which they perceived as endangered by Lincoln's leadership. They contended that the industrially advancing North, wielding increasing political clout, aimed to overrule the agricultural South, destabilizing the core of Southern community life.

On the other side, the Unionists advanced a more pragmatic approach. They warned of the economic fallout of secession, emphasizing Louisiana's crucial trading relationships with Northern states and Europe, facilitated through the bustling port of New Orleans. Breaking away from the Union, they argued, would mean facing blockades, losing essential markets, and risking the state's hard-earned prosperity. Moreover, they highlighted the potential bloodshed, cautioning that a civil war would be costly not just in monetary terms but in human lives.

Despite the fervent Unionist arguments, the convention's momentum veered towards secession. External events played a role in this shift. The secession of deep Southern states like South Carolina, Mississippi, and Florida created a sense of inevitability about the Confederacy's formation. To many in Louisiana, it seemed wiser to join these neighboring states rather than stand against the tide.

Yet, the decision wasn't unanimous. When the vote was eventually called on January 26, 1861, 113 delegates voted in favor of secession, while seventeen voted against it. The state's Ordinance of Secession was adopted, officially severing Louisiana's ties with the Union. As the news spread, reactions were mixed. In many plantation areas, bells rang out in jubilation, and impromptu parades celebrated the perceived victory for states' rights and Southern independence. But in regions with stronger Unionist leanings, especially parts of New Orleans, the mood was somber. Many felt a profound sense of uncertainty about the future.

Louisiana's secession had broader implications for the nation. It sent a strong signal to other Southern states contemplating their next steps. The decision further emboldened Confederate sympathizers while deepening the resolve of the Unionists. More tangibly, Louisiana's secession meant that the Confederacy now had control over the mouth of the Mississippi River, a strategic advantage that would prove significant in the ensuing conflict.

In the months that followed, Louisiana quickly integrated itself into the Confederate apparatus. The state sent representatives to the Confederate Congress and began preparations for potential hostilities. Militias were mobilized, defenses strengthened, especially around New Orleans, and resources were redirected towards the war effort.

But beneath this veneer of Confederate unity, the divisions evident during the secession debate lingered. Many in Louisiana remained deeply apprehensive about the path the state had chosen. As the nation hurtled towards war, Louisiana found itself at the heart of the storm, its internal tensions mirroring the broader national struggle.

Louisiana in War: Battles and Alliances

As the American Civil War erupted in 1861, both the Union and Confederate sides quickly recognized Louisiana's critical position. The Mississippi River, serving as a major channel for trade and communication in the war's Western front, was invaluable. Dominance over this river was akin to having a grip on the nation's core regions. As one of the most populous and economically connected cities in the Confederacy, New Orleans became a focal point in this war.

For the Confederacy, retaining control of Louisiana, especially its waterways and the vital port of New Orleans, was crucial. The state's fertile lands also supplied significant provisions to Confederate forces throughout the South. Recognizing this, Confederate authorities worked swiftly to fortify key positions. Forts Jackson and St. Philip, situated along the Mississippi River below New Orleans, were bolstered, and the Confederate Navy sought to command the river with a fleet of improvised gunboats.

However, the Union also took action. President Lincoln famously stated that the Mississippi "must be held by us at all hazards." Union strategists devised plans to sever the Confederacy in two by capturing the length of the river, a strategy known as the Anaconda Plan. For this to be realized, New Orleans, the "Queen of the South,' had to be captured.

In April 1862, Union Flag Officer David Farragut led a bold naval expedition to take the city. Running his fleet past Forts Jackson and St. Philip under the cover of darkness and a fierce bombardment, Farragut's ships reached New Orleans virtually unopposed. The Confederate lines were circumvented and caught off guard. This, coupled with New Orleans' vulnerability to Farragut's formidable artillery, gave the city no choice but to capitulate. The loss of the South's most prominent city dealt a significant setback to their war ambitions, simultaneously uplifting Northern spirits.

Following the capture of New Orleans, Union forces began a determined push up the Mississippi. Baton Rouge, Louisiana's capital, faced skirmishes, but the pivotal battle in the campaign was the Siege of Port Hudson in 1863. Positioned atop a prominent ridge, Port Hudson remained the final Confederate bastion along the Mississippi. Under the leadership of General Nathaniel P. Banks, Union troops besieged the stronghold for a relentless forty-eight days, marking it as the lengthiest siege in US military records. The defenders held out valiantly, although outnumbered and suffering from malnutrition. However, after hearing of the fall of Vicksburg in July, another Confederate bastion further up the river, the garrison at Port Hudson finally capitulated on July 9, ensuring Union control of the entire Mississippi River and effectively severing the Confederacy in two.

While these significant battles and sieges were unfolding, numerous skirmishes and smaller engagements dotted Louisiana's landscape. The state's vast swamps, bayous, and forests provided ample opportunities for guerrilla warfare. Confederate partisans, utilizing the difficult terrain, continuously harassed Union supply lines and patrols. These engagements, though often overlooked in broader war narratives, played a significant role in diverting Union resources and attention.

One notable resistance group was the "Louisiana Tigers," initially formed as a part of the state militia and later incorporated into the Confederate Army. Though they participated in more conventional battles outside the state, including the Battle of Gettysburg, the spirit they embodied was indicative of the fierce resistance many Louisianans felt towards Union occupation. They were renowned for their aggressive fighting style and, unfortunately, their indiscipline, which sometimes verged on lawlessness.

In addition to these smaller, localized resistances, Louisiana witnessed several full-scale battles after the capture of New Orleans. One such engagement was the Battle of Mansfield in 1864. As Union forces under General Nathaniel P. Banks moved northwestward from the Mississippi River into Louisiana's interior during the Red River Campaign, they sought to establish a deeper foothold in the state, seize cotton stocks, and potentially push into Texas. However, at Mansfield, they met a determined Confederate force commanded by General Richard Taylor, son of former US President Zachary Taylor.

In the ensuing battle, Union troops, stretched thin and caught somewhat off-guard, were pushed back and defeated by Taylor's Confederate force. The setback at Mansfield, combined with logistical challenges and the broader strategic picture—which included Grant's pressing operations in Virginia—led to the Union abandoning the Red River Campaign.

This battle, among others, illuminated a crucial aspect of the Civil War in Louisiana. While the Union might have gained significant strongholds, especially along the Mississippi River, vast swathes of the state's interior remained contested. Despite facing setbacks, the Confederacy could still muster forces and challenge Union operations.

Meanwhile, the waterways of Louisiana remained a vital theater. The extensive bayou and river system provided avenues for both Confederate and Union naval operations. The Confederates utilized makeshift gunboats and the natural advantages of the bayous to launch surprise attacks on Union naval patrols. Conversely, the Union Navy tried to patrol and secure these waterways, ensuring they remained open for logistics and troop movements.

In urban centers, particularly New Orleans, life under Union occupation was challenging. The city, once a hub of Southern culture and commerce, was under tight Union control. Major General Benjamin Butler, who governed the city after its fall, imposed strict regulations. His rule was marked by controversial decisions, including that infamous "Woman Order," which treated any woman showing open disrespect to Union soldiers as a prostitute, causing an outcry among residents and even international condemnation.

Despite its vast swamps and bayous, Louisiana's interior was not spared from the war's devastation. The state's agricultural infrastructure, particularly its cotton industry, bore the brunt of the conflict. Union forces frequently engaged in a scorched-earth policy, destroying crops and infrastructure to cripple the Confederate war effort. Such tactics exacerbated food shortages, leading to economic hardships and civilian suffering.

Yet, it wasn't just military operations and governance that made the war period tumultuous for Louisiana. The very fabric of its society was undergoing transformation. Enslaved Africans, sensing the possibility of liberation, often risked their lives to escape plantations and reach Union lines. For the Confederates, these escapes represented not only a loss of labor but also a symbolic blow to the institution they were fighting to uphold.

These so-called "contrabands" were initially a source of confusion for Union commanders. Some viewed them as spoils of war, while others saw them as persons to be liberated. Over time, many found themselves in contraband camps, places of relative safety (though often rife with disease and poverty). Many would later enlist in the Union Army, seeing combat in the state and beyond.

The utilization of African American troops in the region was groundbreaking. The First Louisiana Native Guard, an all-black regiment comprised primarily of free men of color from New Orleans, was one of the first such units to be recognized by the Union army. Their service challenged preexisting notions of bravery and combat readiness attributed to black soldiers. By the war's end, nearly 24,000 black Louisianans had served in the Union forces, a testament to their commitment to freedom and equality.

On the Confederate side, Louisiana provided vital resources and manpower. Despite suffering setbacks, particularly in the loss of major cities and control of the Mississippi River, the state's soldiers continued to fight valiantly on multiple fronts. Their contribution was not limited to their home state; Louisiana brigades and regiments found themselves in major battles throughout the Confederacy, earning reputations for their combat prowess.

The culmination of the conflict saw a state deeply scarred, its cities in ruins and its society in flux. New Orleans, once a bustling port and cultural epicenter, had seen its trade decimated by blockades and its societal norms upended. Baton Rouge and other towns, repeatedly changing hands, were physically and psychologically battered.

However, within this devastation, new beginnings took root. Slavery, once a bedrock of Louisiana's society before the war, teetered on the edge of dissolution. Having embraced the winds of freedom and demonstrated their valor, the state's African American community stood ready to shape the post-war terrain. For Louisiana, the Civil War's conclusion wasn't merely about ending the conflict; it signaled the birth of a reshaped societal fabric that would be molded during the tumultuous times of Reconstruction.

Rebuilding from Ashes: Reconstruction Challenges

The Civil War's conclusion didn't spell an instant reprieve for Louisiana. If anything, the war's end signaled the onset of fresh hurdles. After enduring years marred by strife and societal turmoil, the state now confronted the daunting mission of mending its tangible landscapes and societal ties. The path of Reconstruction—aimed at weaving the Southern states back into the Union's tapestry—was fraught with intricacies. Louisiana became a poignant symbol of the wider tribulations the South wrestled with.

The Freedmen's Bureau, established by Congress in 1865, played a crucial role in this period of transition. The bureau's agents in Louisiana were given the daunting task of assisting former slaves in their transition to freedom. They had to mediate labor contracts between freedmen and former slave owners, address issues of land redistribution, and provide educational and medical assistance to a population long denied such opportunities. While the bureau's work in Louisiana had tangible successes, notably in establishing schools for African Americans, it also faced resistance from segments of the white population who viewed it as an external imposition on state affairs.

Beyond the economic challenges, Louisiana faced the equally arduous task of political reconstruction. The tug-of-war over political dominion in Louisiana's post-war environment was fraught with tension. Central to this discord was the position and influence of the state's African American community. Though the chains of slavery had been broken, this did not seamlessly translate into comprehensive civil rights. (The new constitution drafted in 1864, while abolishing slavery, stopped short of granting suffrage to black Louisianans.)

The earliest stages of Reconstruction, often labeled "Presidential Reconstruction" under the helm of Presidents Lincoln and Johnson, embraced a more forgiving stance towards reincorporating the South. In Louisiana, this led to a swift reinstatement of civil governance, predominantly steered by those who had shown allegiance to the Confederacy. This era was marked by the introduction of the "Black Codes"—statutes designed to restrict the liberties and entitlements of the freshly-liberated African American populace. This legislation aimed to institutionalize racial disparities, constrict economic avenues for black citizens of Louisiana, and secure a compliant workforce for the state's agricultural estates.

The imposition of these codes, combined with violent acts against African Americans, drew the ire of the Radical Republicans in Congress. For them, such actions underscored the need for a more rigorous approach to reconstruction. Their concerns would eventually lead to the implementation of Congressional or "Radical" Reconstruction in the late 1860s, a period that would see the establishment of new state governments across the South, including Louisiana, that were more inclusive of African American participation and rights.

The opening years of Reconstruction in Louisiana, therefore, were marked by significant tensions. Economic hurdles, political turbulence, and ingrained societal biases melded, forging a whirlwind of dilemmas. As Louisiana endeavored to rise from the war's aftermath, it became a focal point in the nation's discourse about the core essence of American democracy.

Transitioning from the 1860s to the 1870s, Louisiana played a key role in America's quest to delineate the essence and boundaries of its post-war identity. The state's Reconstruction nuances unfolded amidst a tapestry of swift political, societal, and economic evolution.

The 1868 Louisiana Constitution, often referred to as the most progressive post-war Southern constitution, reflected these tumultuous times. It enfranchised African American men, abolished property qualifications for officeholders, and provided for state-funded education—a first in the state's history. This charter paved the way for African Americans to engage in Louisiana's political arena. In a relatively brief period, black citizens of Louisiana ascended to positions in local governance, the state assembly, and even secured seats in the US Congress.

However, these advancements were met with fierce resistance. White supremacist groups, such as the White League in Louisiana, sought to reverse the gains made by African Americans during Reconstruction. They employed violence and intimidation to suppress black voters and challenge Republican governance. The Colfax Massacre of 1873 stands as one of the most egregious examples. Here, in a confrontation over disputed local election results, members of the White League attacked the town's courthouse, resulting in the deaths of several black militia members and civilians. Incidents such as these were not isolated events but part of a coordinated effort to restore white Democratic rule by undermining Republican-led, biracial governance.

Economically, Louisiana underwent a transformation after the war. Before the tumultuous years of conflict, Louisiana's economy thrived primarily through agriculture. But the scars left by the war, intertwined with the newfound freedom of the formerly enslaved, reshaped this economic foundation. Many plantation owners, having sunk their life's savings into an economy anchored by slavery, were confronted with the financial shifts of a changing labor landscape.

The plantation system, although still present, had to adapt to a world without slavery. Sharecropping and tenant farming became prevalent, with many former slaves and impoverished whites entering contractual agreements with landowners. These arrangements, though offering a degree of autonomy, often resulted in cycles of debt and dependency. Coupled with the decline in cotton prices on the international market, Louisiana's agrarian economy grappled with uncertainty and adjustment.

At the same time, the state sought to diversify its economic base. New Orleans, with its strategic location, was primed to become an economic hub. The city witnessed investments in infrastructure, such as railroads, which connected it to national and international markets. These developments, however, often prioritized the interests of the white elite, sidelining the needs and aspirations of the state's African American and poorer white populations.

Societally, Louisiana was a cauldron of change. Schools, particularly those established for African Americans, became centers of hope and progress. Churches played a pivotal role in the African American community, serving as spiritual centers and platforms for political mobilization and community organization. Yet, racial tensions simmered, exacerbated by economic disparities and political power struggles.

At the heart of these tumultuous times stood New Orleans, a city marked by its contrasts. Its rich tapestry of French, Spanish, African, and American heritages thrived, with festivities like Mardi Gras, its distinctive music, and culinary wonders speaking to a possible harmonious coexistence. However, beneath this vibrant exterior, New Orleans grappled with deep-seated divisions rooted in race, wealth, and politics.

The middle phase of Reconstruction in Louisiana was a period of flux. While significant strides were made in advancing the cause of racial equality and economic progress, these gains were continually challenged by deeply entrenched prejudices and powerful interests resistant to change. The state became both a beacon of hope and a stark reminder of the long road ahead for post-war America.

The final phase of Louisiana's Reconstruction era was marked by re-entrenchment and the resurgence of Democratic control. National fatigue over Reconstruction, along with a growing North-South political détente, gave Southern Democrats the leverage they needed to reclaim power.

By the later 1870s, Louisiana's political landscape had undergone significant shifts. The 1877 Compromise, which settled the contentious presidential race between Rutherford B. Hayes and Samuel J. Tilden, bore direct consequences for Louisiana's trajectory. In exchange for Democratic support for Hayes' presidency, federal troops were withdrawn from the South. This removal effectively signaled the end of federal oversight in Louisiana and marked the beginning of the "Redemption" movement. The "Redeemers" were Southern Democrats who championed the restoration of white supremacy and the "old order." In Louisiana, they systematically dismantled the political and civil rights gains made by African Americans during Reconstruction.

The 1879 state constitution, a product of the Redeemer era, drastically rolled back many of the advances of the 1868 constitution. While it didn't overtly revoke the right of African Americans to vote, it instituted numerous voting restrictions, including literacy tests and poll taxes. These mechanisms, often applied subjectively, were designed to disenfranchise black voters. Moreover, the new constitution facilitated gerrymandering (changing the boundaries of the electoral districts to favor a certain party), further reducing African American political influence.

Social dynamics during this period were deeply intertwined with these political and economic shifts. With the Democrats back in power and the federal government largely absent, Louisiana saw an uptick in racial violence. The atrocities committed by groups like the White League became a pervasive terror tactic to maintain racial hierarchy and suppress black aspirations. The legal and extralegal measures to enforce segregation were being solidified, laying the groundwork for the Jim Crow era that would define the late nineteenth and early twentieth centuries in the American South.

Yet, amidst these adversities, the African American community displayed resilience. Black churches continued to play a pivotal role, evolving into safe havens against a backdrop of racial animosity. The African American press emerged as a potent tool, chronicling injustices and galvanizing community action. Black businesses, schools, and mutual aid societies flourished, reflecting a drive to establish self-reliant communities within an increasingly hostile environment.

The end of Louisiana's Reconstruction era, therefore, was a complex tableau. The era became one of setbacks, witnessing the gradual unraveling of the progress achieved during the prior decade. However, this period also showcased the resilience and determination of those aiming for justice and equality amidst formidable challenges. As Louisiana stepped into the twentieth century, the imprints of Reconstruction—its triumphs, shortcomings, and persistent issues—continued to shape the state's historical narrative.

Chapter 6 – Late Nineteenth Century to Early Twentieth Century

As the stormy days of Reconstruction faded, Louisiana stood on the cusp of significant metamorphosis. The transition between the nineteenth and twentieth centuries marked a time of striking evolution, both for Louisiana and the wider United States. With the industrial revolution charging ahead, cities growing and expanding, and America's global footprint deepening, the stage was set for monumental shifts. In the heart of Louisiana, broader national currents took on a unique flavor, shaped by the state's rich history, diverse culture, and distinct environment.

This chapter delves deep into this era of transformation, highlighting how Louisiana grappled with the immense shifts and prospects that emerged in the twilight of the nineteenth century and dawn of the twentieth. By weaving together the economic, social, and global narratives, we aim to chart the journey of a state caught in the whirlwind of a swiftly transforming globe.

From Agriculture to Industry: A Changing Landscape

The economic advancements Louisiana experienced in the closing years of the twentieth century mirrored the wider changes sweeping across the United States. While the North had felt the pulse of the Industrial Revolution earlier on, the South began to embrace this industrial metamorphosis after Reconstruction.

The agrarian system, rooted in the antebellum plantation economy, faced numerous challenges. While cotton remained a dominant crop, its profitability was tempered by fluctuating market prices and recurrent boll weevil infestations. The predominant sharecropping system that had emerged after the Civil War often locked both black and white farmers in cycles of debt and dependency.

The timber industry began to gain prominence, especially in the northern parts of the state. Louisiana's vast pine forests became a valuable resource, driving the growth of lumber mills and creating new towns and communities centered around this burgeoning industry. The swift growth of railroads across the state began bridging the gap between rural locales and bustling urban hubs and ports. This not only eased the transportation of timber but also ushered in fresh economic opportunities.

The discovery of oil and natural gas in the early twentieth century marked another significant turning point. Towns like Jennings witnessed the rush of prospectors and investors eager to tap into the state's vast underground reserves. The oil boom not only diversified Louisiana's economy but also introduced new technologies, workforces, and infrastructural demands.

Parallel to these developments was the rise of manufacturing and industrial production. The strategic port of New Orleans, bolstered by its entrenched trade pathways, blossomed as a nexus for diverse sectors, ranging from ship crafting to culinary processing. Its advantageous position by the Mississippi River amplified its role as a premier locale for merchandise exports, elevating its economic significance.

Yet, the pivot towards industrial prowess came with its own set of hurdles. Transitioning from a farming-centric to an industry-driven economy demanded substantial financial investment, advanced technology, and a workforce with specialized skills—elements that were in short supply at the outset. Still, this economic evolution prompted a significant alteration in labor patterns. The drift of countryside dwellers to city hubs, lured by industrial employment, spurred urban growth and birthed a varied city-based labor force. The surging need for hands in factories, mills, and processing plants opened doors for both genders, though frequently in demanding environments.

As the twentieth century unfolded, the repercussions of this economic transition manifested vividly across Louisiana's environmental and socio-cultural terrains. The waning of the plantation era ushered in an era of land reallotment and varied farming techniques. The rise of compact farms and varied produce, including rice and sugarcane, breathed new life into specific segments of the state's farming domain. Additionally, with the growth of industries, land that was once dedicated to sprawling cotton fields began to host factories, refineries, and railroads.

But as with any period of significant change, there were societal repercussions. The fading of specific farming methods resulted in economic shifts for numerous individuals, compelling them to either embrace the budding industries or chase prospects elsewhere. During this time, a notable number of Louisianans, particularly African Americans, relocated to northern metropolises such as Chicago and Detroit. They were lured by industrial employment and the hope of escaping the racial strains prevalent in the South. While many migrated out, Louisiana's booming industries attracted a new wave of migrants, further diversifying its populace.

Infrastructure also underwent radical changes. The expanding industries necessitated improved transportation and communication networks. The flourishing of rail systems and the evolution of roadways eased the transit of commodities and individuals both within and outside the state. Harbors, notably in New Orleans, underwent advancements and enlargement to cater to the escalating trade, solidifying Louisiana's enduring prominence in domestic and global trade.

Many Louisianans, especially those rooted in agrarian practices, viewed the rise of factories and refineries with suspicion. They mourned the loss of a simpler way of life, fearing the societal implications of unchecked industrial growth.

Environmental concerns also began to emerge. The ecological repercussions of burgeoning industries, particularly the procurement and refinement of natural resources, cast doubts over the enduring health of Louisiana's bountiful natural habitats. Deforestation, pollution of waterways, and the disruption of local habitats became pressing issues, leading to early calls for conservation and sustainable practices.

Labor issues also came to the forefront. As industries expanded, the workforce increasingly sought just wages, improved working conditions, and humane work hours. The closing years of the nineteenth century and the dawn of the twentieth witnessed a surge in labor activism in Louisiana, leading to notable strikes and demonstrations. Labor unions emerged as key entities, bridging the gap between the workers and industry magnates, and were instrumental in influencing the state's labor policies.

Simultaneously, shifts in education mirrored societal changes. Given a growing diverse demographic and the needs of emerging industries, there was a heightened focus on public schooling, vocational education, and advanced academic pursuits. Educational establishments adapted to cater to the demands of an industrializing society, ensuring Louisiana's citizens were armed with the necessary competencies for an evolving economic terrain.

Society in Flux: Demographics, Cities, and Traditions

The transition from the nineteenth to the twentieth century signified a pivotal phase for Louisiana, encompassing sweeping changes in its societal and cultural fabric. This timeframe brought a surge in diverse demographics, urban growth, and a reimagining of the state's cultural heritage, painting a picture of a community in dynamic transformation.

Demographic Shifts

The conclusion of the Civil War and the ensuing Reconstruction era had already instigated profound demographic changes in the state. The end of slavery and the subsequent push to weave former slaves into the South's society had enduring consequences. In Louisiana, the black community started to stake its claim in the political, economic, and cultural arenas, even as it faced deep-rooted prejudice and the rise of Jim Crow regulations.

Parallel to these changes, the late nineteenth century brought waves of European immigrants. Seeking refuge from economic hardships and political turmoil in their homelands, Italians, Germans, and Irish saw Louisiana, with its burgeoning industries and agricultural prospects, as a land of opportunity. These communities found homes in the city and countryside alike. New Orleans emerged as a prime center for Italian and Irish inhabitants. By the dawn of the twentieth century, the makeup of the state's primary urban areas had dramatically shifted from just decades earlier. These European newcomers not only enriched Louisiana's ethnic tapestry but also introduced unique cultural rituals, faiths, and customs.

Furthermore, Louisiana's strategic position along the Gulf Coast made it a focal point for trade and migration from the Caribbean and Central America. This led to a smaller but significant influx of Hispanic and Creole populations, further enhancing the state's multicultural mosaic.

Urban Expansion and Development

This period was also emblematic of a shift from a predominantly agricultural society to an increasingly urbanized one. New Orleans, always a vital port city, experienced exponential growth. The influx of migrants, coupled with industrialization, necessitated urban expansion. Neighborhoods such as the Garden District and Uptown saw significant development, characterized by grand mansions and avenues reflective of the prosperity of the age. However, this growth wasn't limited to the affluent. Working-class neighborhoods like the French Quarter and the Marigny also expanded, housing the myriad of workers flocking to the city for industrial opportunities.

Baton Rouge, Shreveport, and Lafayette, though not as renowned as New Orleans, experienced distinct urban evolutions. These cities blossomed into hubs for trade, academia, and administration, each showcasing a unique fusion of cultures and customs shaped by the varied communities that called them home.

Infrastructure development went hand in hand with urban expansion. The development of streetcars, bridges, and better road networks transformed the way people moved within and between cities.

Cultural Traditions in a Changing Landscape

Louisiana's unique cultural traditions, shaped by centuries of diverse influences, evolved during this period. The infusion of European cultures, especially those of the Italians and Irish, added new layers to the state's already rich cultural diversity. The St. Joseph's Day altars, a Sicilian tradition, became a staple in many communities, symbolizing gratitude and invoking blessings. Likewise, Irish influences became pronounced in New Orleans, with St. Patrick's Day parades and celebrations becoming annual fixtures.

The African American community, while facing systemic prejudices, began to carve out spaces for its cultural and artistic expressions. The birth of jazz in the late nineteenth century epitomized this cultural synthesis. Brass bands, jazz funerals, and the thriving music scene in areas like Congo Square in New Orleans provided a platform for African American artists to showcase their talents and shape American music in profound ways.

The Emergence of Civic Institutions and Societal Norms

As cities expanded and cultures intermingled, Louisiana, like much of the South, grappled with the societal norms that would govern its increasingly diverse populace. This period marked the rise of numerous civic institutions aiming to cater to various societal needs.

Educational institutions played a pivotal role in this new Louisiana. Public schools, especially in urban centers, grew in number and influence. These establishments endeavored to integrate the state's diverse immigrant groups, fostering a shared national identity. Yet, as Jim Crow laws took hold, division became institutionalized, resulting in the creation of distinct schools for African Americans. These schools frequently faced financial shortfalls and were deprived of crucial resources.

Religious institutions also underwent transformation. While Catholicism, deeply rooted in Louisiana's history, retained its prominence, other Christian denominations brought by European immigrants and African American communities began establishing their foothold. Synagogues, indicative of a small but influential Jewish community, also found their place in the state's religious landscape.

Concurrently, the turn from the nineteenth to the twentieth century marked a rise in communal societies and groups. Entities such as the Freemasons, the Knights of Pythias, and mutual aid groups became integral in various communities, delivering socio-economic benefits to their affiliates. Within the African American community, bodies like The National Association for the Advancement of Colored People (NAACP) emerged as powerful forces, championing civil rights and countering racial prejudice.

Press, Publications, and the Spread of Ideas

The press played a monumental role in shaping societal narratives during this period. Newspapers in English and other languages proliferated, providing communities with news, entertainment, and a sense of identity. *The Times-Picayune* in New Orleans and other regional publications provided detailed accounts of local, national, and international events, molding public opinion and giving voice to various societal segments.

Literature and arts likewise mirrored the state's diverse influences. Writers hailing from Louisiana, such as Kate Chopin, began gaining national attention, their works reflecting the complexities and nuances of

Southern society.

The Age of Festivals and Celebrations

One of the most vivid representations of Louisiana's societal flux was the evolution of festivals and public celebrations. Mardi Gras, with roots in French Catholic traditions, transformed into a statewide extravaganza, drawing influences from various communities. Parades, balls, and public festivities became more elaborate, with Krewes representing different societal groups, from the elite Rex and Comus to the African American Zulu.

Juneteenth, marking the emancipation of slaves, gained prominence within the African American community, symbolizing freedom, resilience, and hope. European festivals, like the Italian Tarantella or the German Oktoberfest, found their place in the state's annual calendar, celebrating the heritage and contributions of these communities.

Louisiana at the Cusp of Modernity

As the twentieth century unveiled itself, Louisiana was on the brink of a modern era. Shifting from its agricultural roots, it showcased urban hubs, multifaceted communities, and adaptive cultural norms. The fusion of European, African, Native American, and various other legacies had cultivated a society unparalleled in its depth and intricacy.

Nevertheless, the path was fraught with obstacles. The lingering effects of Jim Crow, economic inequalities, and deep-rooted biases remained evident. Amidst this backdrop, the foundations for future revolutions, which would confront established norms and advocate for a diverse and fair Louisiana, began to take root. Consequently, the closing years of the nineteenth century and the onset of the twentieth prepared Louisiana for momentous changes in the coming years, charting its course towards a future once deemed beyond reach.

The Global Context: Louisiana through Two World Wars

At the beginning of the twentieth century, global occurrences left an unforgettable mark on the United States, and Louisiana found itself intricately woven into this larger picture. The colossal upheavals of the world wars, which reshaped the international landscape, deeply influenced Louisiana in tangible and subtle ways. Louisiana's geopolitical significance, economic transformation, and the ever-changing socio-cultural fabric were overwhelmingly influenced by these global confrontations.

Louisiana's Geopolitical Significance

Louisiana's position as a major port state made it strategically vital to the United States during both world wars. The Mississippi River, culminating in the bustling port of New Orleans, remained a significant artery for transporting goods, troops, and resources. The Port of New Orleans, already a central hub for trade, saw its importance skyrocket yet again as wartime logistics and shipping needs grew. The US military recognized the state's strategic value. As a result, numerous military bases and facilities were established or expanded throughout Louisiana.

World War I, while distant, had its implications for Louisiana. As the US entered the war in 1917, the state saw a surge in enlistment, with thousands of Louisianans joining the armed forces. Simultaneously, wartime demands stimulated local industries. Shipbuilding, timber, and oil industries, among others, experienced a boom as they catered to national and international needs.

The Socio-Economic Impacts of the Wars

The ripple effects of the global wars were deeply felt in Louisiana's economy. The state's agricultural sector, especially cotton farming, suffered during World War I due to disrupted European markets and labor shortages. This decline was counterbalanced by the rise of other sectors. The discovery of oil in the state in the early twentieth century dovetailed with the increased industrial demands of the war, transforming Louisiana's economy. Thus, towns like Jennings and Shreveport became focal points of this burgeoning oil industry.

World War II further accelerated these changes. The demand for war materials resulted in a surge of jobs and growth in the industrial and manufacturing sectors. Higgins Industries in New Orleans, for instance, became renowned for its production of Higgins boats, landing crafts that played a pivotal role in amphibious assaults, most notably during D-Day.

Yet, even as these wars galvanized parts of the economy, they also illuminated and intensified underlying racial and socio-economic divides. African Americans, despite their substantial contributions to the war both in combat and on the home front, remained ensnared in a web of systemic prejudice and segregation. Nevertheless, these wars inadvertently planted the kernels of transformation.

The Cultural Interplay during the Wars

While Louisiana's economic landscape underwent significant shifts during the world wars, the cultural realm also saw substantial developments. The state's diverse population meant that the wars, especially World War I, were viewed through multifaceted lenses. The sizable German and Italian communities in Louisiana faced suspicion and, at times, outright hostility, given their home countries' global alignments. Many were subjected to internment or faced other restrictions during both wars, particularly World War II.

Conversely, the wars also brought an influx of people and ideas to Louisiana. Troops from different parts of the country, stationed in Louisiana or passing through its ports, introduced new cultural elements, which in turn influenced local traditions and norms. Jazz, already a burgeoning musical form in New Orleans, was carried by troops and sailors to various parts of the world, serving as an unofficial soundtrack to the American war effort. The global resonance of this uniquely Louisiana-born music solidified the state's reputation as a cultural melting pot.

Reshaping the Political Landscape

The wars inevitably brought changes to Louisiana's political environment. The increased federal involvement in the state, as a result of military installations and defense contracts, strengthened the influence of the national government. As America positioned itself as a global superpower post-World War II, the ramifications on local politics were significant. Federal defense spending brought economic prosperity but also placed Louisiana more firmly under the scrutiny and regulation of the central government.

Moreover, the wars, particularly World War II, stirred democratic ideals among residents. The fight against oppressive regimes overseas highlighted the contradictions at home, particularly concerning civil rights. These war years, in essence, sowed the early seeds for the civil rights movement that would crescendo in the 1950s and 60s.

Economic Realignment and Post-War Boom

Post-World War II, Louisiana experienced an economic transformation, continuing its shift from agriculture to industry. The state's oil and petrochemical industry expanded dramatically, bringing in a flood of investments and making Louisiana one of the nation's primary energy hubs. Cities like Baton Rouge and Lake Charles benefited immensely from these developments, seeing their populations and economies grow.

However, this industrial growth came with environmental costs. The construction of canals and the infrastructure for oil and gas exploration intensified coastal erosion issues. Balancing economic growth with environmental preservation emerged as a pivotal dilemma for Louisiana as the twentieth century progressed.

Cultural Evolution and Legacy of the Wars

Post-war, Louisiana saw a cultural renaissance. The shared experience of the wars acted as a catalyst, bringing together diverse communities. The influx of servicemen from various regions exposed Louisianans to diverse cultures, ideologies, and customs. This influence was especially pronounced in music, art, and literature.

Yet, it was also a period of introspection. As the state grappled with its place in this new globalized world, there was a revival of interest in preserving Louisiana's unique heritage. Efforts to document and promote Creole and Cajun cultures, languages, and traditions gained momentum. Festivals, museums, and educational programs were established, celebrating the state's rich and diverse history.

Chapter 7 – Civil Rights Movement

The struggle for civil rights that surged through the mid-1900s marks a defining chapter in the story of America, with voices rising in unison for equality and justice. Against a backdrop painted by centuries of colonial rule, the echoes of slavery, and the lingering divisions of the Civil War, Louisiana emerged as a crucial arena in this nationwide push for change. The state's particular demographic and political makeup meant that its civil rights struggles often had distinctive characteristics, even as they mirrored the broader efforts taking place throughout the South.

In the bayous, streets of New Orleans, and state institutions, Louisiana's civil rights activists faced vehement opposition and sometimes violent repression. Yet, their determination and sacrifices laid the groundwork for significant changes in the state and beyond. This chapter explores Louisiana's role in the civil rights movement, focusing on early resistance, key moments of change, and the legacy this period left for future generations. Through stories of courage and perseverance, we see a state grappling with its past while striving for a more inclusive future.

Storm Before the Calm: Early Struggles

Understanding the civil rights movement in Louisiana requires a recognition of the historical precursors that set the stage for mid-twentieth-century activism. The state's long history of racial segregation, deeply embedded in its societal fabric, made any attempts at dismantling this structure perilous.

Post-Reconstruction Louisiana, like much of the American South, devised a systematic approach to marginalizing its black population. The rolling out of "Black Codes" followed by the rigid Jim Crow laws etched a deep line of division across the everyday lives of Louisianans, creating separations in schools, on buses, and throughout public life. These rules were not just lines in law books; they were stark declarations of who held power and who was forced to the margins. Coupled with this legal entrenchment of racism, violent intimidation tactics, such as lynching, were frequently employed to maintain white supremacy and curtail any semblance of black resistance or assertion.

But resistance did emerge, sometimes subtly and, at times, overtly. During the dawn of the twentieth century, African American communities took a stand to carve out their voice within the societal narrative. A pivotal development was the founding of Black-owned publications, such as the *Louisiana Weekly*, which rolled off the presses in 1925, becoming a beacon for the African American perspective and challenging the established order. Such publications provided an essential platform for African American voices to disseminate news about racial injustices and foster a sense of community and shared purpose among the black populace.

Parallel to these efforts were the early legal challenges. At the same time, a pivotal moment unfolded in the fight against educational segregation. In 1936, an African American hopeful, Lloyd Gaines, knocked on the doors of Missouri State University's law school, seeking to gain admission and thereby challenging the entrenched barriers of segregation. Gaines was denied entry due to his race, but his case would eventually pave the way for the landmark *Brown v. Board of Education* decision nearly two decades later. Though Gaines tragically went missing before seeing the fruits of his struggle, his efforts highlighted the deep-seated institutional racism in the country's education system.

Grassroots efforts began taking shape in Louisiana's urban and rural areas alike. In places like Baton Rouge, African Americans initiated boycotts against segregated bus services as early as 1953.

The challenges faced by these early activists cannot be understated. Opponents of desegregation wielded significant power in Louisiana, both politically and socially. White Citizens' Councils emerged in response to black activism, aimed at maintaining segregation through economic intimidation and other forms of pressure. These groups, alongside the Ku Klux Klan (KKK), represented the fierce headwinds against which early civil rights activists had to fight.

The latter part of the 1930s and 1940s witnessed an acceleration in organized efforts towards racial equality in Louisiana. With World War II underway, African Americans from Louisiana, like those across the nation, enlisted in significant numbers, fighting for democracy abroad while being denied basic rights at home. The dichotomy was palpable and further catalyzed the desire for change.

Many returning Black veterans became vocal advocates for civil rights. Returning home as heroes, yet still consigned to the margins of society, these veterans refused to settle quietly into the shadows of second-class status. Their call for dignity and equal rights echoed through a nation beginning to awaken to the profound injustices of racial discrimination, particularly in the era that followed the war's end.

Labor movements became crucial platforms for addressing racial discrimination in Louisiana. The Brotherhood of Sleeping Car Porters emerged as a formidable force for racial and labor justice. This union, led by Black employees, passionately advocated for improved wages and conditions and, importantly, fought to dismantle the segregation within its industry. Its concerted efforts and demonstrations brought to light the dual burdens of racial discrimination and economic exploitation, marking a significant chapter in the fight for equitable treatment in the workplace.

The sway of major civil rights entities increasingly resonated throughout Louisiana. The NAACP stood at the forefront, wielding significant influence in the concerted effort to dismantle segregationist policies. This organization's strategic legal challenges and advocacy played a pivotal role in the state's civil rights landscape and the broader movement for racial equality. One notable instance was the fight against the white primary system, which effectively excluded black citizens from the democratic process. The NAACP's legal victory in *Smith v. Allwright* (1944) was a watershed moment, outlawing white primaries and reaffirming the voting rights of black Louisianans.

Churches, long-standing pillars of the Black community in Louisiana, amplified their role as centers of resistance. Clergy like the Reverend T.J. Jemison of Baton Rouge used the pulpit to spread the message of civil rights and organized and participated in direct actions like boycotts and sit-ins. These religious institutions offered spaces for strategizing, mobilizing, and fostering a spirit of community resilience.

Yet, every advance was met with fierce resistance. White supremacists responded to black activism with heightened violence. Bombings, threats, and physical assaults became distressingly common, aimed at intimidating activists and black communities at large. The murder of activists, both black and white, underscored the grave risks associated with challenging the deeply entrenched racial hierarchy of Louisiana.

Despite their formidable challenges, the champions of early civil rights movements in Louisiana remained resolute. The younger generation began to emerge as a force for change, with students from the state's historically black colleges and universities joining their peers nationwide in sit-ins, freedom rides, and efforts to register voters.

As the 1950s came to a close, the early endeavors of these activists in Louisiana had planted the seeds for more expansive movements to come. Each act of mobilization, legal challenge, new institution, and act of steadfast resistance contributed to a strong foundation. This groundwork would pave the way for the sweeping actions and significant transformations that the 1960s would usher in.

Landmarks of Change: Key Movements in Louisiana

The 1960s were pivotal in the civil rights movement's trajectory. Louisiana, with its unique sociocultural backdrop, became a significant theater of struggle and change. The state's battles for racial equality can be encapsulated by a series of landmark events, each shedding light on the broader movement's dimensions.

1. The Baton Rouge Bus Boycott (1953)

Even before the famed Montgomery Bus Boycott galvanized the nation, Baton Rouge provided a precursor, demonstrating the potency of organized black resistance. The roots of this boycott can be traced to the unfair segregated seating system on city buses. Black passengers were required to pay at the front, exit the bus, and then re-enter from the rear door to occupy seats in the designated "colored" section. Inspired by a recent Supreme Court ruling that declared segregated seating on interstate buses unconstitutional, the Reverend T.J. Jemison, organized a boycott of the city's buses. For eight days in June 1953, black residents of Baton Rouge refrained from using the buses, relying instead on an organized carpool system. This boycott resulted in a compromise: while buses remained segregated, the humiliating procedure of paying at the front and entering from the back was eliminated, and black passengers could occupy any vacant seat from the back forward. This early victory, though modest, offered a blueprint for future mass mobilizations.

2. New Orleans School Desegregation (1960)

The national mandate to desegregate schools after the *Brown v. Board of Education* decision of 1954 met with considerable resistance in the South. Louisiana was no exception. In 1960, New Orleans became a focal point of this resistance when four young black girls, notably Ruby Bridges, enrolled at previously all-white schools. Their admission was met with violent mobs, vehement protests, and even school closures by defiant state officials. The courage of these children, especially Bridges, who faced the vitriol of segregationists daily as she entered William Frantz Elementary School, became symbolic of the deep-seated racism in educational institutions and the bravery required to confront it.

3. The Southern University Protests (1972)

In 1972, Southern University in Baton Rouge emerged as a focal point for student activism, reflecting a larger surge of black student advocacy throughout the nation. The student body's protests were fueled by deeper currents of discontent—a yearning for improved educational resources, the removal of law enforcement from the campus, and a stronger voice in the administrative decisions of the university. These students did not stand alone; they were part of a nationwide call for change, signaling a new chapter in the fight for equality and justice within academic institutions. Tensions reached a climax in November when law enforcement clashed violently with students, resulting in the tragic deaths of two young protestors, Denver Smith and Leonard Brown. Their deaths, though devastating, brought national attention to the grievances of black students and sparked a renewed push for substantive changes in educational institutions.

4. Bogalusa Civil Rights March (1967)

Bogalusa, Louisiana, although small, encapsulated the immense challenges and struggles that defined the civil rights movement across the South. Notoriously marred by rampant racism and the pervasive influence of the Ku Klux Klan, the town stood as a stark symbol of the fierce resistance civil rights activists faced in their quest for equality and justice. In 1967, a civil rights march was organized from Bogalusa to Baton Rouge, demanding federal intervention against racial violence and the enforcement of voting rights. The march, led by A.Z. Young, president of the Bogalusa Voters and Civic League, covered 105 miles in six days. Despite facing threats and intimidation, the marchers' determination culminated in a massive rally at the state capitol in Baton Rouge.

5. The Voter Registration Push

Louisiana's suffrage landscape for African Americans in the early 1960s was marked by a shocking blend of systematic suppression and intimidation. The path to the ballot box in Louisiana was fraught with daunting barriers for black citizens. Legal hurdles such as literacy tests and poll taxes, along with the shadow of violence from vigilante groups like the KKK, turned the act of registering to vote into an act of bravery and defiance. Against this backdrop, organizations like the Congress of Racial Equality (CORE) and the Southern Christian Leadership Conference (SCLC) took a stand. They launched determined voter registration drives, underlining the crucial link between political engagement and the pursuit of freedom and rights. While the efforts faced hostility, including the assassination of Wharlest Jackson in Natchez after his promotion to a "white" job in 1967, the campaigns bore fruit. By the mid-1960s, black voter registration began to increase, albeit slowly, laying the foundation for more representative local governance in subsequent decades.

6. The Role of the Free Southern Theater

Cultural institutions played an underrated yet vital role in the civil rights movement. The Free Southern Theater, founded in 1963 by John O'Neal, Doris Derby, and Gilbert Moses, emerged as a formidable tool for activism in Louisiana. With a commitment to producing plays that spoke to the black experience in the South, the theater toured rural areas, bringing performances that combined art, education, and activism. Their productions were not just entertainment but avenues for community discussions on race, justice, and freedom. By utilizing art as a medium for mobilization, the Free Southern Theater added a vibrant cultural dimension to Louisiana's civil rights struggles.

7. Challenging White Supremacy in St. Landry Parish

St. Landry Parish in the late 1960s exemplified the volatile mix of white supremacist sentiment and black resistance. Here, local chapters of the Deacons for Defense and Justice, an armed black self-defense group, emerged in response to white terrorist violence. The Deacons provided security for civil rights workers, escorted black children to recently desegregated schools, and protected black communities from Klan violence. The decision to take up arms was rarely about aggression; it was a necessary strategy for self-defense amidst the constant looming threats to their lives and liberties. The unwavering stance and measures taken by African Americans in Louisiana were a profound declaration of their resolve to secure their safety and rights.

8. Louisiana's Pivotal Lawsuits and Legal Milestones

Beyond grassroots movements and direct actions, Louisiana's journey toward racial equality was punctuated by significant legal battles. In *Hall v. St. Helena Parish School Board* (1961), for instance, the US Fifth Circuit Court of Appeals ordered the immediate desegregation of public schools in the parish. In another landmark case, *United States v. Louisiana* (1974), the Department of Justice successfully challenged Louisiana's multi-member legislative districts, arguing they diluted black voting strength. The aftermath of these legal victories reshaped Louisiana's political and educational landscapes, advancing desegregation and ensuring more equitable representation.

9. Black Panther Party in New Orleans

The Black Panther Party's influence extended to Louisiana. Established in 1970, the New Orleans chapter focused on community programs, including free breakfast initiatives for children and health clinics. While the party faced consistent police harassment and surveillance, its work underscored the blend of social welfare and political activism that defined the Black Panthers. The engagement of African Americans in Louisiana mirrored the evolving direction of the civil rights movement during the late '60s and early '70s, broadening the lens to confront deep-rooted socio-economic inequalities.

These events and initiatives, spread across a turbulent decade, underscore Louisiana's distinct place within the broader American civil rights movement. While the state shared many of the South's racial dynamics, its history, demographics, and culture created unique challenges and opportunities for civil rights activists. Whether through legal battles, direct action, cultural initiatives, or political mobilization, Louisiana's black community showcased resilience, innovation, and a relentless pursuit of justice.

Echoes of the Past, Hopes for the Future

In Louisiana, the civil rights movement surpassed mere protests and courtroom struggles—it was a sweeping social and cultural shift. With the arrival of the 1970s, the legacy of this movement resonated powerfully, shaping dreams and desires for a more equitable society. The movement's influence was lasting, steering the state's social transformation and underscoring the enduring hurdles to true equality.

The Persistence of Memory

It's essential to understand that while landmark legislation and court decisions made during the civil rights era addressed systemic racism, they could not instantly alter individual prejudices or societal norms. Louisiana, with its storied past of French, Spanish, British, and African influences, faced the challenge of reconciling its historical identity with its modern aspirations. Memorials, museums, and oral history projects began to emerge, capturing the narratives of those who had fought for equality. These testimonies, both poignant and harrowing, served as a testament to the state's tumultuous journey towards justice.

Education – The Great Equalizer

With the desegregation of schools legally mandated, the focus shifted to ensuring equitable access to quality education. African American communities in Louisiana sought not just integration but a curriculum that accurately represented their history and contributions. As the tides of change washed over Louisiana, schools started weaving the threads of black history into their educational curricula. Historically black colleges and universities (HBCUs) such as Southern University and Grambling State University stood at the forefront of this academic renaissance. These bastions of African American education consistently nurtured a lineage of leaders, intellectuals, and change-makers who were instrumental in carving out the state's tomorrow.

Political Representation and the Rise of Black Leadership

The voter registration drives of the 1960s bore fruit in the subsequent decade. As more African Americans became eligible to vote, Louisiana began to witness a surge in black political representation. Ernest "Dutch" Morial, elected in 1977, became New Orleans' first black mayor, signaling a shift in the political landscape. His tenure, which prioritized urban development and education, exemplified the changing dynamics of power in the state. At the state level, the increased representation of African Americans in the Louisiana State Legislature reflected the broader transformation in the racial makeup of American politics.

Economic Aspirations and Challenges

With legal barriers dismantled, the pursuit of economic prosperity became paramount for Louisiana's black community. However, systemic issues persisted. In the heartland of Louisiana, particularly in its more remote corners, African American communities were wrestling with the historical tendencies of economic marginalization. Concerted efforts emerged to turn the tide, championing black entrepreneurship and pioneering pathways toward fair economic participation. Initiatives sprouted, aiming to plant seeds of prosperity where there had once been barren fields of opportunity. Yet, despite these endeavors, disparities in wealth, employment, and business ownership remained, underscoring the depth of structural inequalities.

Cultural Renaissance and Celebration

One of the most vibrant outcomes of the post-civil rights era in Louisiana was the cultural renaissance within the African American community. Music, art, literature, and festivals flourished, celebrating the rich tapestry of black Louisiana. Long rooted in the streets of New Orleans, jazz witnessed a revival, with artists infusing contemporary influences into this classic genre. Mardi Gras, a long-standing tradition, began to incorporate themes and narratives from the civil rights movement, turning the festival into a platform for celebration and reflection.

Civil Rights Tourism and Memory Preservation

As the twentieth century waned and the new millennium beckoned, Louisiana embraced its role as a repository of significant civil rights landmarks. Sites of protests, schools central to desegregation efforts, and churches that once hosted meetings became attractions for those keen on understanding the movement's history. The state recognized the dual potential of these sites for education and tourism, working diligently to ensure they were preserved and accessible. The creation of the Louisiana Civil Rights Trail in the late twentieth century was a testament to this commitment, guiding visitors and residents through pivotal locations and events that changed the course of the state's history.

Continued Challenges and Modern Advocacy

Despite significant strides, the quest for equality was far from complete. Instances of racial profiling, economic disparities, and debates over representation in media and education reminded Louisianans that the struggle was ongoing. Contemporary activists drew inspiration from their predecessors, combining traditional protest methods and modern tools like social media. This era witnessed the emergence of new movements and organizations dedicated to addressing systemic racism and promoting justice, reflecting the evolving nature of civil rights advocacy.

Diversity - Louisiana's Changing Demographics

By the close of the twentieth century, Louisiana's cultural quilt became even more detailed and intricate with new threads from distant lands. People journeyed from the corners of Latin America, the diverse expanses of Asia, and the varied landscapes of Africa, each bringing a piece of their world to the bayou state. These newcomers wove their traditions, flavors, and dreams into the state's already rich mosaic. These communities also faced challenges reminiscent of earlier civil rights struggles. Their endeavors to establish themselves, seek representation, and integrate into Louisiana's social fabric presented both obstacles and opportunities for the broader movement for inclusivity.

Environmental Justice and Civil Rights

Louisiana's unique geographical position made it susceptible to environmental challenges, notably hurricanes and coastal erosion. Historically marginalized communities often bore the brunt of these environmental crises. As awareness grew around environmental issues, a new dimension was added to Louisiana's ongoing civil rights discourse. Activists started to underline the interconnectedness of environmental health and social justice, pointing out how minority communities were often unfairly burdened by environmental hazards. This emerging concept of environmental justice emphasized that a clean and safe environment is a fundamental right for all, cutting across lines of race and economic status.

Looking Forward - The Legacy of the Civil Rights Movement

Entering the twenty-first century, Louisiana still deeply felt the influence of the civil rights movement. Educational facilities, public buildings, and various landmarks took on the names of prominent figures of the civil rights era from the local community and the nation, serving as enduring reminders of the struggles and triumphs of the movement. Annual commemorations and events served as reminders of the sacrifices and victories while emphasizing the work still ahead. The younger generation, equipped with the histories of their forebears and the tools of modern activism, stood poised to continue the fight for a just and equitable Louisiana.

Chapter 8 – Modern Louisiana

At the cusp of the twenty-first century, Louisiana found itself not only a repository of a deep and varied historical past but also a state pulsating with modern energy. The narratives of prior centuries—those of exploration, conflict, cultural synthesis, economic evolution, and societal change—merged to form the rich culture that characterized the modern Louisiana identity. But with this historical consciousness, Louisiana also faced a series of challenges and opportunities that would further shape its path forward.

This modern era for Louisiana was marked by significant economic diversification, the necessity of resilience against natural adversities, and a continued commitment to its vibrant and globally recognized cultural expressions. While deeply rooted in its historical journey, each of these facets encapsulated Louisiana's contemporary essence.

In this chapter, we will explore the multifaceted dimensions of modern Louisiana: a state forging ahead in the contemporary world while continually drawing strength and identity from its rich history. From the bustling energy hubs of the Gulf to the vibrant streets during Mardi Gras, Louisiana's present is as captivating as its past.

From Oil Rigs to Jazz Bars: Diverse Economies

The economic tapestry of modern Louisiana, while richly textured by its historical industries, has been notably shaped by two seemingly disparate forces: the oil industry and its cultural heritage, especially jazz. Understanding the juxtaposition of these two elements requires a dive into the twentieth century, when Louisiana's economic landscape began a shift that positioned it prominently on both national and global stages.

The Rise of Oil

The early twentieth century witnessed a critical shift in Louisiana's economic foundation with the discovery of oil. The Jennings Field, uncovered in 1901, signaled the state's foray into the oil industry, setting the stage for further exploration and discovery. As the years progressed, Louisiana found itself dotted with wells, and by the mid-twentieth century, the Gulf of Mexico emerged as a hub for offshore drilling activities. This development cemented Louisiana's role as an integral part of the United States' oil and gas sector.

This shift towards petroleum reshaped the state's economic profile, physical landscape, and demographics. Towns that once thrived on agriculture began to see a surge in population as workers flocked to oil fields and refineries. Cities like Baton Rouge and Lafayette became pivotal industrial hubs, with refineries, pipelines, and petrochemical plants dotting their outskirts. The economic boom brought about by the oil industry was palpable. Job opportunities expanded, and the state's GDP grew significantly. Louisiana's ports, already historically significant, became crucial exit points for American oil, making them some of the busiest in the nation.

However, this heavy reliance on the oil sector was not without its pitfalls. The oil industry, inherently volatile due to global market dynamics, led to periods of boom and bust for Louisiana. The state's economy became tethered to the global price of oil, leading to economic downturns in periods of low oil prices, most notably in the 1980s.

Jazz: An Economic Symphony

While oil dominated the industrial narrative, another form of liquid gold—jazz—was coursing through Louisiana's veins. In the early twentieth century, New Orleans was already setting the stage as a vibrant center of music. As the decades unfolded, this city's rhythm and blues filled its storied streets and echoed beyond its borders, establishing New Orleans as a renowned hub for jazz enthusiasts worldwide by the latter half of the century. The rise of jazz clubs, festivals, and music schools solidified the city's reputation.

Jazz's economic impact on Louisiana, while not as immediately tangible as the oil rigs and refineries, was nonetheless significant. Tourism boomed as aficionados from around the world flocked to the state, eager to experience authentic jazz in its homeland. This influx of visitors bolstered other sectors of the economy, from hospitality to retail.

The cultural economy, with jazz at its forefront, became one of Louisiana's unique selling points. Festivals like the New Orleans Jazz & Heritage Festival celebrated the state's musical heritage and generated hundreds of millions of dollars in economic impact annually.

In this duality of oil and jazz, Louisiana showcased its capacity to innovate while cherishing its roots. The melding of these economies, one rooted in the ground and the other in culture, set Louisiana apart, crafting an economic narrative as diverse as its history.

Diversifying the Portfolio: Oil's Complementary Industries

As the oil industry began to burgeon, ancillary sectors also experienced growth. The need for advanced machinery, infrastructure, and technology meant a rise in manufacturing jobs and establishments. The intricate network of pipelines required to transport oil and gas across the state and to other parts of the country fostered a secondary industry focused on construction, maintenance, and monitoring. Furthermore, the ports of Louisiana, particularly the Port of New Orleans and the Port of South Louisiana, saw a marked increase in activity, handling vast amounts of exported crude oil and imported equipment. The state, recognized for its strategic location and extensive river system, capitalized on its assets to develop a robust shipping and maritime economy.

However, it wasn't just the physical movement and extraction of oil that bolstered Louisiana's economy. The business of oil—ranging from brokerage to futures trading—brought an increase in white-collar jobs. Cities, especially New Orleans, saw an influx of corporate offices and headquarters of major oil and petrochemical companies. This emergence of corporate culture added another layer to Louisiana's diverse economic landscape, creating a blend of blue-collar refinery workers and white-collar executives, all driven by the energy sector's heartbeat.

Jazz's Cultural Offshoots

While jazz was Louisiana's musical crown jewel, its influence catalyzed the appreciation and development of other cultural forms. Jazz clubs weren't the only hotspots lighting up the cultural landscape of New Orleans. Alongside these hubs of smooth brass and syncopated rhythms, venues dedicated to blues, R&B, and the rising tide of rock 'n' roll also found their footing. The French Quarter, with its wrought-iron balconies and cobblestone streets, turned into a melting pot for these diverse musical expressions. However, the artistic renaissance in the Big Easy wasn't confined to music. The excitement and energy around Louisiana's cultural scene sparked a renaissance in visual arts, theatre, and literature, each drawing inspiration from the state's rich history and diverse demographic makeup.

A significant offshoot of this cultural boom was the culinary explosion in Louisiana. While the state's cuisine, with its Creole and Cajun flavors, was always a point of pride, the influx of tourists and the global spotlight on its cultural scene made Louisiana's food not just a local delight but an international sensation. Restaurants, food festivals, and culinary schools experienced unprecedented growth. The economic implications were manifold: local produce and seafood industries saw increased demand, and culinary tourism began to feature prominently in the state's economic development plans.

Confluence of Two Titans

As the mid-twentieth century unfolded, Louisiana stood at a pivotal junction of industry and influence. The state's rich oil reserves had catapulted it into the spotlight, securing its place as a cornerstone in the United States' energy sector and granting it a substantial voice in the nation's economic and political arenas. Simultaneously, its rich cultural heritage, especially jazz, made it a global ambassador for American arts. This duality was not without its challenges. The environmental impact of the oil industry often clashed with the state's image as a cultural haven. Pollution, particularly in waterways, threatened local wildlife and impacted sectors like fisheries, which were crucial for the economy and the state's culinary reputation.

Yet, Louisiana, with its knack for resilience and adaptability, constantly sought to strike a balance. Investment in cleaner technologies in the oil sector, conservation efforts, and a keen emphasis on sustainable tourism ensured that both these pillars of the state's economy could coexist. The dance between oil rigs and jazz bars was a delicate one, but it was a testament to Louisiana's enduring spirit and its commitment to progress without forsaking its roots.

When Nature Strikes: Disasters and Resilience

Louisiana's location along the Gulf Coast has historically exposed it to the whims of nature, particularly the hurricanes that gather strength over the Gulf of Mexico. Yet, the story of Louisiana is not solely one of weathering storms; it's a narrative steeped in the tenacity and flexibility of its people. The state's annals are marked by a profound determination to stand firm, rebuild, and thrive despite the recurrent onslaught of natural disasters.

Early Encounters and Lessons

Louisiana's trysts with hurricanes can be traced back to the early settlement days, with storms periodically shaping the destiny of its communities. As early as the eighteenth century, colonists learned the brutal power of nature. Situated in a low-lying region with a sprawling delta, the state's terrain made it susceptible to the powerful winds of hurricanes and the perilous storm surges they ushered. While early settlers lacked the technological advancements of modern times, they quickly understood the importance of strategic positioning, elevating structures, and establishing robust communication networks.

In the nineteenth century, the state grappled with some significant hurricanes. Each storm brought its own set of challenges, from the destruction of infrastructure to the loss of life and property. Yet, with every disaster, invaluable lessons were learned. Local communities began implementing rudimentary warning systems, and there was a greater emphasis on community preparedness. Over time, buildings were constructed to be sturdier, with some towns relocating to higher grounds to minimize flood risks.

Twentieth Century: A Period of Transformation

At the turn of the twentieth century, Louisiana was at the heart of a transformative period characterized by swift technological progress and a move towards urban living. New Orleans was a prime example of this shift, transforming into a thriving city teeming with new residents and advancing infrastructure. But with growth came challenges, especially when managing the natural threats the state had always faced.

The hurricane of 1965, Hurricane Betsy, was a watershed moment for Louisiana. Striking as a Category 4 storm, Betsy inundated parts of New Orleans, leaving much of the city underwater and causing billions in damage. It was a grim reminder of the state's vulnerabilities. However, Betsy also acted as a catalyst for change. Recognizing the need for a robust defense mechanism against such calamities, the city accelerated its efforts to improve the levee systems and flood control measures.

This commitment to safeguarding the state against natural threats was tested time and again. In the latter half of the century, hurricanes like

Camille (1969) and Andrew (1992) posed significant challenges. But the lessons from Betsy and the subsequent infrastructure improvements meant the state was better prepared to tackle them.

While technological advancements, improved forecasting, and enhanced preparedness reduced the immediate impact of these storms, there remained an undeniable truth: Louisiana's relationship with nature was a complex interplay of respect, preparation, and recovery. The state's historical resilience would soon be tested in unprecedented ways as it entered the new millennium.

Twenty-first Century: Facing Unprecedented Challenges

With the dawn of the twenty-first century, Louisiana found itself contending with increasingly intense and frequent meteorological events, a trend in line with global observations of the impact of climate change. The correlation between rising global temperatures and heightened hurricane activity became a grave concern for the state. This was especially troubling for a region that relied so heavily on its coastlines for economic activities such as fishing, oil extraction, and cultural sustenance, as seen in its vibrant coastal communities.

The year 2005 brought a chilling reality to the forefront with Hurricane Katrina, a tempest that would etch its name into the annals of history for its sheer destructiveness. Striking Louisiana as a Category 3 hurricane, Katrina's wrath was unparalleled. The storm's intensity, combined with a tragically ill-prepared levee system in New Orleans, resulted in breaches that inundated 80 percent of the city. The damages were not restricted to infrastructure alone. Over a thousand lives were lost, and the socio-economic fabric of the region faced severe disruptions. Katrina exposed vulnerabilities in both physical defenses and emergency response systems.

The aftermath of Katrina was a period of introspection. There were pressing questions regarding urban planning, especially in flood-prone regions, and the future of New Orleans itself. The disaster drew international attention, and support poured in from all quarters. The recovery process was arduous, with residents determined to rebuild their lives and the city. The spirit of community, so intrinsic to Louisiana's ethos, became its guiding light. Neighbors helped neighbors, and volunteers from across the nation descended on the state to assist in the rebuilding process.

Katrina's devastation underscored the importance of climate resiliency. Louisiana, working hand-in-hand with federal bodies, launched significant initiatives to strengthen its protective measures against natural disasters. This joint effort resulted in the creation of the Hurricane and Storm Damage Risk Reduction System, a $14.6 billion project engineered by the US Army Corps of Engineers. This ambitious system stretches over 133 miles and consists of an array of levees, floodwalls, surge barriers, and pump stations, all built to safeguard New Orleans from the devastating effects of storm surges.

Yet, as Louisiana fortified its defenses against hurricanes, another disaster loomed on the horizon. In 2010, the Deepwater Horizon oil spill cast a spotlight on Louisiana's environmental and economic fragility, although it was a man-made catastrophe rather than a natural one. This disaster resulted in millions of barrels of oil pouring into the Gulf of Mexico, inflicting severe damage on marine ecosystems, crippling the local fishing trade, and tarnishing the state's precious coastal margins.

Combating these catastrophes emphasized an undeniable reality: while physical infrastructures like levees and regulations could be strengthened, the spirit of resilience was Louisiana's most potent asset. The shared history of overcoming adversities, whether wrought by nature or human error, instilled a sense of unity and determination in its residents.

As the century progressed, Louisiana continued to face its share of challenges. From Hurricane Rita in 2005 to Barry in 2019, each event, while harrowing, also reaffirmed the state's commitment to resilience and preparedness. These trials, more than anything, exemplified Louisiana's enduring spirit and its unwavering determination to rise, rebuild, and rejuvenate.

Mardi Gras, Gumbo, and Jazz: Living Culture

In the face of adversity and change, cultural constants have a way of grounding communities and forging identity. For Louisiana, a state with a mosaic of influences ranging from French and Spanish to African and Native American, the tapestry of its living culture has remained vibrant and evocative. This cultural persistence has been manifested most iconically through Mardi Gras, gumbo, and jazz—each a symbol of the state's rich heritage and an emblem of Louisiana's undying spirit.

Mardi Gras: A Historic Carnival

Mardi Gras, translated as "Fat Tuesday," has roots in medieval Europe but has been celebrated in Louisiana since the eighteenth century. It is the day before Ash Wednesday, marking the onset of Lent in the Christian calendar—a period of reflection and abstinence. Before the calm of Lent descends, Louisiana becomes the heart of jubilation, especially during Mardi Gras. Tracing its roots to 1699, the state's Mardi Gras history began when French explorers Pierre Le Moyne d'Iberville and Sieur de Bienville landed near what is now New Orleans, christening it "Pointe du Mardi Gras" after the festivities of the same name in France. As years passed, the local celebrations took on a life of their own, intertwining the customs of French, Spanish, and African cultures.

By the nineteenth century, Mardi Gras had transformed into an extravaganza of color and excitement, replete with ornate balls and vibrant parades. "Krewes," or social clubs, began to form, each responsible for organizing individual parades and balls. The Mistick Krewe of Comus, formed in 1856, was the first of these, pioneering the use of themed floats—a tradition still followed. Today, the city bursts into a riot of colors, with masks, beads, and flamboyant costumes, each Krewe bringing its unique flair to the proceedings.

Yet, Mardi Gras is not just about the grandeur and festivity. Beneath the colorful facade, it is a testament to the state's diverse heritage. The incorporation of masked balls from French traditions, the flamboyant parades reminiscent of Spanish festivals, and the profound influence of African rhythms and dance moves in the celebrations reflect Louisiana's multicultural lineage.

Gumbo: The Melting Pot of Flavors

If Mardi Gras is the visual representation of Louisiana's culture, gumbo is its gastronomic emblem. This hearty stew is more than just a dish; it's a narrative of the state's history, told through flavors and ingredients.

Originating from West African cooking traditions, gumbo was adopted and adapted by Louisiana's settlers. As different communities made Louisiana their home, gumbo evolved. The French introduced roux, a mixture of flour and fat, as the base. Spanish influence brought tomatoes; Native Americans introduced filé, ground sassafras leaves.

Each pot of gumbo tells a story. Whether it's seafood gumbo brimming with shrimp, crab, and oysters—a nod to Louisiana's bountiful coastlines—or chicken and sausage gumbo, each version speaks of the state's varied landscape and mosaic of cultures. Communal cooking, sharing, and enjoying gumbo has become a Louisiana tradition bridging generations and backgrounds.

It All Comes Back to Jazz

Arguably, the most transcendent of Louisiana's cultural contributions, jazz, is not just a genre of music but a profound reflection of the state's soul and complexity. An amalgamation of African rhythms, blues, ragtime, and European classical music, Jazz is both structured and improvisational, mirroring the fluidity and dynamism of Louisiana itself.

Legendary figures like Buddy Bolden, often referred to as the first jazz musician, began to popularize this new sound at the turn of the century. Louis Armstrong, hailing from New Orleans, rose to be the emblem of jazz itself. His unique raspy singing and masterful trumpet skills lifted jazz from the local scene of New Orleans and placed it under the international spotlight. Armstrong's musical journey, which unfolded over five prolific decades from the Roaring Twenties through the Swinging Sixties, didn't just redefine jazz; it left an indelible mark on the entire landscape of American popular music.

Jazz clubs, especially those in the historic French Quarter and on the storied Basin Street, became the heartbeats of the city. Places like Preservation Hall, opened in 1961, were not just venues but institutions dedicated to keeping the jazz tradition alive. Over time, as musicians traveled and the Great Migration saw a movement of African Americans to the North, jazz evolved and diversified, leading to the birth of subgenres like bebop, swing, and cool jazz. Yet, its heart remained firmly in Louisiana.

It is not just the notes and rhythms that make jazz the quintessential Louisiana music. It is the ethos. Jazz, with its emphasis on individual expression within a collective, mirrors the spirit of Louisiana—a place where individual cultures retain their uniqueness but contribute to a larger, richer tapestry. The improvisational nature of jazz speaks to Louisiana's resilience and adaptability, its ability to innovate and evolve in the face of challenges.

Chapter 9 – Louisiana's Cultural Mosaic

Few states in the US can rival the rich cultural tapestry of Louisiana, a place where traditions from distant lands have interwoven so intimately that they have birthed entirely new cultures, dialects, and cuisines. The very essence of Louisiana, with its meandering bayous and storied streets, has been shaped by centuries of diverse influences—from European settlers and African slaves to Native Americans and Asian immigrants. Each group has left indelible marks, making Louisiana more than just a geographical entity; it stands as a testament to the power of cultural convergence and the beauty of shared histories.

It's essential to delve deep into this intricate weave to fully appreciate the state's unique identity. By examining its cultural origins and tracing the paths of influence, we can better understand the present-day celebrations, music, art, and flavors that make Louisiana truly singular. The stories of Creole and Cajun communities exemplify the blending and evolution of traditions, making them significant focal points of this exploration.

In this chapter, we're tracing the journey of diverse communities and their cultural contributions and delving into the shared heritages that shape Louisiana's modern identity. The state's ability to absorb, adapt, and innovate ensures that while it honors its past, it continually reshapes its cultural future.

Melting Pot of Traditions: Origins and Influences

Louisiana's distinction as a cultural cauldron is not a recent development; it is deeply rooted in its early history, as we've already explored. The state's unique geographical location made it a coveted piece of land for colonial powers, but with these territorial ambitions came people—settlers, explorers, and enslaved individuals, each bringing their own traditions, beliefs, and practices. Since we've already covered a lot of the state's history, let's recap the additions to the melting pot that is Louisiana.

The Native American tribes, such as the Choctaw, Caddo, and Natchez, were the original inhabitants. Their presence in the region dates back millennia. These tribes cultivated the land, navigated its intricate waterways, and established intricate societal structures. Their deep connection to the environment influenced their belief systems, rituals, and daily practices, laying the foundation of Louisiana's cultural fabric.

Then came the Europeans. Spanish explorers were among the first to navigate the region in the early sixteenth century, but it was the French who left a lasting cultural mark. When Robert Cavelier, Sieur de La Salle, claimed the region for France, a new chapter of cultural infusion opened. French settlers brought their language, customs, legal systems, and Catholicism. This Gallic influence remains evident today in everything from Louisiana's legal system, based on the Napoleonic Code, to the French Quarter of New Orleans, a vibrant hub of cultural festivities.

The eighteenth century brought with it another wave of change. The Atlantic slave trade introduced a large African population to the region. Forced into a harsh life, these individuals maintained and adapted their rich cultural traditions, languages, and spiritual beliefs. Over time, these African traditions melded with local customs, synthesizing practices. The legacy of this blending can be seen in the state's music, from the rhythmic beats of zydeco to the soulful strains of the blues, and in its culinary arts, where African cooking techniques and ingredients added depth and complexity to local dishes.

The nineteenth century marked the onset of another influential era. As the United States expanded westward, English-speaking American settlers and immigrants from various parts of Europe, including the Irish, Germans, and Italians, began to make Louisiana their home. Each brought distinct traditions and influences, further adding to the cultural mosaic. The Germans, for instance, introduced advanced agricultural practices and sausage-making techniques. The Italians, especially the Sicilians, contributed their farming skills and distinctive cuisines to the food industry.

Louisiana's cultural landscape is not solely a product of transatlantic influences. The state has a significant Hispanic community, primarily tracing its roots to the Canary Islands, or Isleños. These settlers, arriving in the late eighteenth century, established communities like San Bernardo and Galveztown. Their unique Spanish dialect, traditions, and folklore remain an integral part of Louisiana's cultural tapestry.

As the timelines progressed, each group that called Louisiana home added to its ever-evolving cultural identity. From music and food to festivals and crafts, the influences of these diverse communities are both distinct and intermingled, making Louisiana a living testament to the power and beauty of cultural amalgamation.

Creole, Cajun, and the Shared Heritage

Louisiana's rich tapestry of cultures reaches its pinnacle in the stories of the Creoles and the Cajuns. These two groups, often intertwined in popular imagination, represent distinct historical, cultural, and linguistic traditions. Their shared geographical space in Louisiana has led to cross-cultural exchanges, yet they maintain identities that are as vivid as they are diverse.

Creole Origins and Influence

The term "Creole" has seen various definitions over the centuries. In its earliest use, it denoted people of European descent who were born in the New World. The French word *créole* has its roots in the Portuguese *crioulo*, referring to a servant raised in one's household. As colonial enterprises expanded, so did the term's scope. In Louisiana, it began to encompass not just the locally born French and Spanish but African, Native American, and mixed-race individuals. The multi-ethnic nature of Creole identity is mirrored in its culture.

New Orleans stands as the symbolic Creole city. The architecture of the French Quarter reflects a design ethos influenced by French, Spanish, and African elements. Creole cuisine, celebrated for its rich flavors and complex techniques, combines French sophistication with African vibrancy and local produce. Dishes like gumbo, étouffée, and jambalaya are testaments to this blend. The Creole tradition is also deeply musical, contributing to the birth of jazz.

Louisiana Creole, though less spoken today, also played a pivotal role. Efforts are in place to revitalize this unique linguistic heritage, signifying its importance in the Creole identity.

Cajun Roots and Resilience

The Cajuns' story is one of enduring perseverance and cultural adaptation. The name "Cajun" is derived from "Acadian," pointing to the French settlers in the northeastern stretches of North America, most notably in what is now Nova Scotia. In the mid-1700s, following the British conquest of Acadia, the Acadians who spoke French were forcibly removed from their lands in a traumatic episode known as the Great Upheaval, or "Le Grand Dérangement" in French. Many Acadians wandered in exile, with a significant number eventually finding refuge in Louisiana's swamplands and bayous.

In these remote terrains, the Cajuns cultivated a life insulated from urban influences. They became adept at navigating the wetlands, leading to a lifestyle deeply connected with the land and waters. Their music, a reflection of their joys and sorrows, gave birth to genres like Cajun folk and zydeco, marked by the lively notes of accordions and washboards.

Cajun French became the lingua franca of these communities. The language, an echo of the old Acadian French, evolved by integrating terms from Spanish, Native American, and English languages. Like the Creoles, Cajuns have a rich culinary legacy. Their food, though rooted in French culinary traditions, was adapted to the local environment. Crawfish boils, boudin (a type of sausage), and dishes using game meats reflect their resourcefulness and proximity to nature.

Shared Spaces and Interactions

While Creoles and Cajuns maintained distinct identities, their shared geography in Louisiana meant that interaction was inevitable. Over time, this led to a fascinating interplay of cultures. Creole and Cajun musicians often played together, leading to a melding of musical styles. There were also exchanges in cuisine. While both groups cherished gumbo, variations in preparation and ingredients often delineated its Creole or Cajun origins.

The Mardi Gras, a festival deeply embedded in Louisiana's cultural psyche, sees both Creole and Cajun representations. While the urban Mardi Gras parades of New Orleans are replete with Creole influences, the rural areas of Louisiana witness the Cajun Mardi Gras, a more traditional celebration marked by costumes, horseback riding, and communal gatherings.

While originating from different historical trajectories, the stories of the Creoles and Cajuns intersect in the shared space of Louisiana. Their resilience in preserving their unique identities, even while blending in certain cultural aspects, highlights the multifaceted nature of Louisiana's heritage. The Creole-Cajun tapestry, woven with threads of adversity, migration, creativity, and interaction, forms an integral chapter in the larger narrative of Louisiana's cultural mosaic. Through their traditions, languages, food, and music, they offer a window into the soul of a state that has always thrived on diversity and unity in equal measure.

Conclusion

As we stand at the crossroads of the past and the future, looking back on Louisiana's multifaceted history offers an opportunity for reflection and understanding. The land, bearing imprints of Native American tribes, European colonizers, African slaves, and a slew of immigrants, tells a story not merely of a state but of humanity's resilience, adaptability, and perpetual search for identity.

From the misty legends of the Native peoples to the ambitious pursuits of European settlers, from the rise of plantations shadowed by the chains of slavery to the soulful rhythms of jazz echoing through New Orleans, Louisiana's history is a symphony. Each note, though distinct, contributes to a larger, harmonious narrative. The tribulations faced, the battles fought, the cultures melded, and the identities formed are all threads in the rich tapestry that is Louisiana.

The bayous and wetlands have witnessed the struggles of the Acadians, turning adversity into a thriving Cajun culture. The streets of New Orleans have echoed with Creole French, encapsulating centuries of cultural amalgamation. The plantations, bearing the dark stain of slavery, have also seen the rise of abolitionist movements and the eventual embrace of civil rights. Through hurricanes and wars, economic depressions and societal upheavals, Louisiana has not just endured; it has evolved, adapted, and grown.

This journey has also been a testament to the state's role as a melting pot of cultures. The interplay of French, Spanish, African, Native American, and many other influences has birthed an unparalleled cultural and social milieu. This intermingling, though sometimes fraught with tensions, has more often led to enriching exchanges and a shared heritage that's uniquely Louisianan.

Louisiana's Evolving Role in America

In the broader tapestry of American history, Louisiana has consistently held a position of significance. From the geopolitics of the Louisiana Purchase, placing vast territories under American governance, to the strategic importance of New Orleans in trade and commerce, Louisiana's contribution to shaping the nation cannot be understated.

But beyond geopolitics and economics, Louisiana's true contribution lies in its cultural legacy. In a nation that prides itself on being a melting pot, Louisiana stands out as a vivid example. Jazz, arguably America's greatest cultural export, has its roots deeply embedded in the Creole and African traditions of Louisiana. The state's culinary contributions, too, have found enthusiasts far and wide. Dishes like gumbo, jambalaya, and crawfish étouffée are not just representative of Louisiana; they've become emblematic of American Southern cuisine.

Furthermore, Louisiana's history with civil rights, from the early rumblings of abolition to the tumultuous 1960s, mirrors the nation's larger struggle with racial inequality. The state, with its complex racial dynamics, became a focal point for discussions on race, segregation, and the path to equality. The battles fought on Louisiana soil, both literal and metaphorical, have shaped national policies and sentiments.

As America confronts modern trials, from the ongoing dialogue on racial equality to the urgent concerns of climate change and the preservation of cultural identity, Louisiana serves as a profound case study. The state's historical journey through racial integration, current battles with increasingly severe natural disasters influenced by a changing climate, and relentless dedication to safeguarding a diverse cultural legacy all offer wisdom that is not merely pertinent but imperative for shaping the nation's path ahead.

In an era of rapid globalization, where local identities can often get subsumed by a broader homogenization, Louisiana stands as a beacon of cultural preservation. Its festivals, traditions, music, and food continue to be celebrated with gusto, offering a template for how regions can retain their unique character in the face of global pressures.

Louisiana is not just a state; it's a story. A story of people, places, events, and emotions. As we close this chapter, it's essential to reflect upon this narrative not as a static entity but as an evolving continuum. The state, with its ever-adaptable spirit, will face new challenges, forge fresh alliances, and discover novel facets of its identity. But through all these shifts, one thing remains certain—the indomitable spirit of Louisiana, forged through centuries of trials and triumphs, will endure and shine.

If you enjoyed this book, a review on Amazon would be greatly appreciated because it would mean a lot to hear from you.

To leave a review:

1. Open your camera app.
2. Point your mobile device at the QR code.
3. The review page will appear in your web browser.

Thanks for your support!

Here's another book by Captivating History that you might like

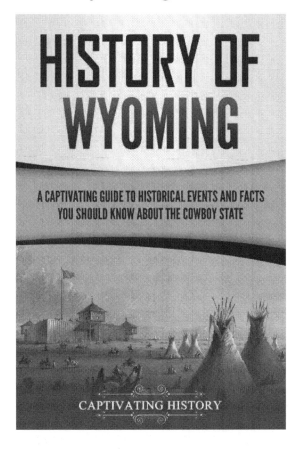

Free Bonus from Captivating History (Available for a Limited time)

Hi History Lovers!

Now you have a chance to join our exclusive history list so you can get your first history ebook for free as well as discounts and a potential to get more history books for free! Simply visit the link below to join.

Captivatinghistory.com/ebook

Also, make sure to follow us on Facebook, Twitter and Youtube by searching for Captivating History.

Resources

Chapter 1

"Native American Tribes of Louisiana" http://www.native-languages.org/louisiana.htm Accessed: October 4, 2023

"American Indians in Louisiana" https://www.nps.gov/jela/learn/historyculture/native-americans-in-louisiana.htm Accessed: October 4, 2023

"Choctaw Heritage of Louisiana and Mississippi" https://www.louisianafolklife.org/lt/articles_essays/choctaw_hert.html Accessed: October 4, 2023

"The Natchez Indians" http://archeology.uark.edu/indiansofarkansas/printerfriendly.html?pageName=The%20Natchez%20Indians Accessed October 4, 2023

"The Natchez Indians" https://www.mshistorynow.mdah.ms.gov/issue/the-natchez-indians Accessed: October 4, 2023

"Early Caddo History" https://www.nps.gov/elte/learn/historyculture/caddo-early-history.htm Accessed: October 4, 2023

"Who We Are" https://mycaddonation.com/history-1 Accessed: October 4, 2023

"Hernando de Soto" https://www.history.com/topics/exploration/hernando-de-soto Accessed: October 4, 2023

"René-Robert Cavelier, Sieur de La Salle" https://www.biography.com/history-culture/rene-robert-cavelier-sieur-de-la-salle Accessed: October 4, 2023

Chapter 2

"René-Robert Cavelier, Sieur de La Salle" https://www.biography.com/history-culture/rene-robert-cavelier-sieur-de-la-salle Accessed: October 4, 2023

"Immigration and Settlement" https://scphistory.org/immigrationandsettlement/#:~:text=In%201698%2C%20nobleman%20Pierre%20le,outpost%20near%20the%20Mississippi%20River. Accessed: October 6, 2023

Woods, Patricia, 1978. "The French and the Natchez Indians in Louisiana: 1700-1731" *Louisiana History: The Journal of the Louisiana Historical Association.* 19(4). Pp. 413-435.

"The Code Noir and the Missouri Compromise" https://www.nps.gov/articles/000/the-code-noir-and-the-missouri-compromise.htm Accessed: October 6, 2023

"The French in New Orleans" https://www.history.com/topics/immigration/the-french-in-new-orleans Accessed: October 6, 2023

"French Colonial Louisiana" https://64parishes.org/entry/french-colonial-louisiana Accessed: October 6, 2023

"A History of New Orleans" https://localhistories.org/a-history-of-new-orleans/ Accessed: October 6, 2023

"Treaty of Fontainebleau" https://64parishes.org/entry/the-treaty-of-fontainebleau-2 Accessed: October 6, 2023

"Treaty of Paris, 1783" https://2001-2009.state.gov/r/pa/ho/time/ar/14313.htm#:~:text=The%20Treaty%20of%20Paris%20was,the%20U.S.%20significant%20western%20territory. Accessed: October 6, 2023

"Antonio de Ulloa y de la Torre Guiral" https://64parishes.org/entry/antonio-de-ulloa-y-de-la-torre-guiral Accessed: October 6, 2023

"Spanish Colonial Louisiana" https://64parishes.org/entry/spanish-colonial-louisiana-adaptation Accessed: October 7, 2023

"Isleños" https://64parishes.org/entry/islenos-adaptation Accessed: October 7, 2023

"Slavery in Spanish Colonial Louisiana" https://64parishes.org/entry/slavery-in-spanish-colonial-louisiana Accessed: October 7, 2023

"Battle of Baton Rouge/ August 5th 1862" https://americanhistory.si.edu/collections/search/object/nmah_325510 Accessed: October 7, 2023

"Third Treaty of San Ildefonso" https://64parishes.org/entry/third-treaty-of-san-ildefonso Accessed: October 7, 2023

"The British Period (1763-1784)"

https://www.nps.gov/foma/learn/historyculture/the-british-period.htm Accessed: October 7, 2023

Chapter 3

"Napoleonic Code" https://64parishes.org/entry/napoleonic-code Accessed: October 9, 2023

"How the Louisiana Purchase Changed the World" https://www.smithsonianmag.com/history/how-the-louisiana-purchase-changed-the-world-79715124/ Accessed: October 9, 2023

"Louisiana Purchase Treaty (1803)" https://www.archives.gov/milestone-documents/louisiana-purchase-treaty Accessed: October 9, 2023

"The United States and the Haitian Revolution, 1791–1804" https://history.state.gov/milestones/1784-1800/haitian-rev#:~:text=on%20the%20colony.-,St.,began%20on%20August%2022%2C%201791 Accessed: October 9, 2023

"Missouri Compromise 1820" https://www.archives.gov/milestone-documents/missouri-compromise#:~:text=This%20legislation%20admitted%20Missouri%20as,remainder%20of%20the%20Louisiana%20Territory Accessed: October 9, 2023

Chapter 4

"Antebellum Louisiana" https://64parishes.org/entry/antebellum-louisiana Accessed: October 11, 2023

"Antebellum Louisiana: Agrarian Life" https://www.crt.state.la.us/louisiana-state-museum/online-exhibits/the-cabildo/antebellum-louisiana-agrarian-life/index Accessed: October 11, 2023

"Plantation Slavery in Antebellum Louisiana" https://64parishes.org/entry/plantation-slavery-in-antebellum-louisiana Accessed: October 11, 2023

"Sugar Plantations in Louisiana" https://talltimbers.org/wp-content/uploads/2014/03/Rehder1979_op.pdf Accessed: October 11, 2023

"Free People of Color in Louisiana" https://lib.lsu.edu/sites/all/files/sc/fpoc/ Accessed: October 11, 2023

"The Free People of Color of Pre-Civil War New Orleans" https://daily.jstor.org/the-free-people-of-color-of-pre-civil-war-new-orleans/ Accessed: October 11, 2023

"Creole History and Culture" https://www.nps.gov/cari/learn/historyculture/creole-history-and-culture.htm#:~:text=In%20colonial%20Louisiana%20the%20term,periods%2C%20regardless%20of%20their%20ethnicity Accessed: October 11, 2023

"Andry's Rebellion (1811)" https://www.blackpast.org/african-american-history/andry-s-rebellion-1811/ Accessed: October 11, 2023

"General Butler and the Woman Order" https://archive.nytimes.com/opinionator.blogs.nytimes.com/2012/06/18/general-butler-and-the-women/ Accessed: October 11, 2023

"New Orleans in the Civil War" https://www.battlefields.org/learn/articles/new-orleans-civil-war Accessed: October 11, 2023

"Louisiana's Secession from the Union" https://64parishes.org/entry/louisianas-secession-from-the-union-adaptation#:~:text=On%20January%2026%2C%201861%2C%20Louisiana,to%20secede%20from%20the%20Union Accessed: October 11, 2023

"Louisiana Civil War" https://www.crt.state.la.us/louisiana-state-museum/online-exhibits/the-cabildo/the-civil-war/index Accessed: October 13, 2023

"Civil War Louisiana" https://64parishes.org/entry/civil-war-louisiana Accessed: October 13, 2023

"Reconstruction: A State Divided" https://www.crt.state.la.us/louisiana-state-museum/online-exhibits/the-cabildo/reconstruction-a-state-divided/index Accessed: October 13, 2023

"Reconstruction" https://64parishes.org/entry/reconstruction Accessed: October 13, 2023

"Guerrilla Warfare in Civil War Louisiana" https://64parishes.org/entry/guerrilla-warfare-in-civil-war-louisiana Accessed: October 13, 2023

"Louisiana Tigers During the Civil War" https://64parishes.org/entry/louisiana-tigers-during-the-civil-war#:~:text=The%20nickname%20originated%20with%20one,known%20as%20the%20Louisiana%20Tigers Accessed: October 13, 2023

"The Freedman's Bureau" https://www.archives.gov/research/african-americans/freedmens-bureau Accessed: October 14, 2023

"Louisiana Constitution of 1868" https://64parishes.org/entry/louisiana-constitution-of-1868 Accessed: October 14, 2023

"The 1873 Colfax Massacre Set Back the Reconstruction Era" https://www.smithsonianmag.com/smart-news/1873-colfax-massacre-crippled-reconstruction-180958746/ Accessed: October 14, 2023

"Louisiana Constitutions" https://64parishes.org/entry/louisiana-constitutions Accessed: October 14, 2023

Chapter 5

"World War II Industrialization in Louisiana"
https://64parishes.org/entry/world-war-ii-industrialization-in-louisiana Accessed:
October 16, 2023

"New Orleans: A Timeline of Economic History"
https://richcampanella.com/wp-
content/uploads/2020/02/article_Campanella_New-Orleans-Timeline-of-
Economic-History_NOBA.pdf Accessed: October 16, 2023

"Reconstruction II: Change and Continuity in Daily Life"
https://www.crt.state.la.us/louisiana-state-museum/online-exhibits/the-
cabildo/reconstruction-change-and-continuity-in-daily-life/index Accessed:
October 16, 2023

"Jim Crow & Segregation" https://64parishes.org/entry/jim-crowsegregation
Accessed: October 16, 2023

"The Power of Leaving: Black Agency and the Great Migration in Louisiana,
1890 – 1939"
https://scholarworks.uno.edu/cgi/viewcontent.cgi?article=1099&context=honors
_theses Accessed: October 16, 2023

"Legacy of Great Migration of black people from the South lives on, speakers
say" https://www.nola.com/news/legacy-of-great-migration-of-black-people-from-
the-south-lives-on-speakers-say/article_0dc3a162-f86b-57ad-b52c-
e2b13ff9a719.html Accessed: October 16, 2023

"New Orleans During the Second World War"
https://www.nationalww2museum.org/war/articles/new-orleans-second-world-
war Accessed: October 16, 2023

"13 Ways World War I Touched New Orleans"
https://www.hnoc.org/publications/first-draft/13-ways-world-war-i-touched-new-
orleans Accessed: October 16, 2023

Chapter 6

"The Black Code of St. Landry's Parish, Louisiana, 1865" https://www.ruhr-
uni-bochum.de/gna/Quellensammlung/05/05_blackcode_1865.htm Accessed:
October 18, 2023

"The Southern "Black Codes" of 1865-66" https://www.crf-usa.org/brown-v-
board-50th-anniversary/southern-black-codes.html Accessed: October 18, 2023

Hebert, Mary Jacqueline, "Beyond Black and White: the Civil Rights
Movement in Baton Rouge, Louisiana, 1945–1972." (1999). *LSU Historical
Dissertations and Theses.* 7045.
https://repository.lsu.edu/gradschool_disstheses/7045

"Montgomery Bus Boycott" https://www.history.com/topics/black-
history/montgomery-bus-boycott Accessed: October 18, 2023

"Baton Rouge Bus Boycott" https://64parishes.org/entry/baton-rouge-bus-boycott Accessed: October 18, 2023

"Brotherhood of Sleeping Car Porters (1925-1978)" https://www.blackpast.org/african-american-history/brotherhood-sleeping-car-porters-1925-1978/ Accessed: October 18, 2023

"Rev. Dr. T.J. Jemison Sr." https://lapoliticalmuseum.com/inductee/rev-dr-t-j-jemison-sr/ Accessed: October 18, 2023

"Ruby Bridges: the six-year-old who defied a mob and desegregated her school" https://www.theguardian.com/society/2021/may/06/ruby-bridges-the-six-year-old-who-defied-a-mob-and-desegregated-her-school Accessed: October 18, 2023

"New Orleans School Crisis" https://64parishes.org/entry/new-orleans-school-crisis Accessed: October 18, 2023

"Taking a Stand" https://64parishes.org/taking-a-stand Accessed: October 18, 2023

"One of the longest marches of the civil rights movement is honored in Louisiana" https://www.cnn.com/2021/08/10/us/louisiana-civil-rights-trail-new-trnd/index.html Accessed: October 18, 2023

"Cold Case: The night Wharlest Jackson was murdered — Feb. 27, 1967" https://www.hannapub.com/concordiasentinel/frank_morris_murder/cold-case-the-night-wharlest-jackson-was-murdered-feb-27-1967/article_82df3dc8-41ad-11e3-b604-0019bb30f31a.html Accessed: October 18, 2023

Fabre, Genevieve, 1983. "The Free Southern Theatre, 1963-1979" *Black American Literature Forum* 17:2. Pp. 55-59

"Deacons for Defense and Justice" https://www.blackpast.org/african-american-history/deacons-defense-and-justice/ Accessed: October 18, 2023

"Louisiana Civil Rights Trail" https://www.louisianacivilrightstrail.com Accessed: October 18, 2023

Chapter 7

"History of Oil & Gas in Louisiana and the Gulf Coast Region" https://www.dnr.louisiana.gov/assets/TAD/education/BGBB/6/la_oil.html#:~:text=In%20September%2C%201901%2C%20the%20first,up%20one%20after%20the%20other Accessed: October 20, 2023

"Oil and Gas Industry in Louisiana" https://64parishes.org/entry/oil-and-gas-industry-in-louisiana Accessed: October 20, 2023

"Jazz Origins in New Orleans" https://www.nps.gov/jazz/learn/historyculture/history_early.htm Accessed: October 20, 2023

"Louisiana Hurricane History"

https://www.weather.gov/media/lch/events/lahurricanehistory.pdf Accessed: October 20, 2023

"Deepwater Horizon Oil Spill" https://coastal.la.gov/deepwater-horizon-oil-spill-content/oil-spill-overview/ Accessed: October 20, 2023

"Mardi Gras 2024" https://www.history.com/topics/holidays/mardi-gras Accessed: October 20, 2023

"A Short History of Gumbo" https://www.southernfoodways.org/interview/a-short-history-of-gumbo/ Accessed: October 20, 2023

Chapter 8

"Creole Culture in New Orleans, Louisiana" https://library.csun.edu/SCA/Peek-in-the-Stacks/creole Accessed: October 22, 2023

"Creoles in Louisiana History" https://seventhcoalition.org/2018/01/22/creoles-in-louisiana-history/ Accessed: October 22, 2023

"From Acadian to Cajun" https://www.nps.gov/jela/learn/historyculture/from-acadian-to-cajun.htm Accessed: October 22, 2023

"Cajuns" https://64parishes.org/entry/cajuns Accessed: October 22, 2023

Made in the USA
Columbia, SC
06 March 2025

54769163R00061